TALES FROM HIGH BLUFF

The Great Outdoors

MATT JOLLEY

This book is a work of fiction. The characters, incidents and dialogue are drawn from the author's imaginations and are not to be construed as real or pertaining to a real event. Any resemblance to actual events or persons, living or dead, is entirely coincidental.

All rights reserved. No part of this book may be used or reproduced in any manner whatsoever without written permission except in the case of brief quotations embodied in critical articles and reviews.

ISBN 13: 978-1-951543-38-9

Library of Congress Control Number:

2025911060

Copyright 2025 © Matt Jolley

Cover by Creative Dolan Design Studio
www.creativedolan.com

DANCING CROWS
PRESS

Printed in the United States

To the Citizens of High Bluff, and the friends who probably wish I hadn't paid attention — again.

Introduction

Welcome Back to High Bluff.

This little book is the second in what's become, for better or worse, a love letter to my cherished hometown. *Tales From High Bluff – The Great Outdoors* picks up right where *Stories My Grandfather Would Like and Other Pleasant Lies* left off—with the same familiar characters, the same dusty streets, and the same big sky overhead. But this time, every story is aimed square at the great outdoors.

Now, I don't mean just hunting and fishing (though there's plenty of that). I'm talking dinosaur chickens, pheasant hunts gone sideways, campfires that double as trash cannons, and yes, even the annual outdoor singing Christmas tree that somehow still manages to stand up every December, despite the odds and the wind. Each tale is written with deep affection—for the land that raised me, and the folks who never gave up on me, no matter how many times I gave them reason to.

A hometown, you see, is the place where you're allowed to make your worst mistakes and still find a soft bed and a warm smile waiting when you come crawling back. The neighbors might still talk about you behind your back—**and sometimes loudly**—but if you ever find yourself in a life-or-death showdown with a man-eating boll weevil, there's a good chance that old friend of yours won't run. And if he does, well—he's probably just grabbing a camera.

Now, here comes the legal bit again: I'll swear up and down that everything in these pages is pure fiction, especially the characters. But if you've spent any time in South Texas, you'll know the difference between bull chips and clumped dirt. And that, dear reader, is the real fun of it.

Happy reading, y'all.

~Matt Jolley

CHAPTER 1

JANUARY

THE PHEASANT HUNT

The cold hill country air stung his lungs but Bull Harlan pressed on across the frost covered field. My dad, Jim, was right behind him, and, this year, Reverend C. Lewis Arbuckle was in tow. The good Reverend decided last November during the Baptist Men's Group annual "How to Carve a Turkey Like Your Grandfather" luncheon he wanted to be more involved with the men of the church.

"Hey there, Jimbo … and uh … Mr. Bull, would ya'll mind terribly if I tag along on next year's pheasant hunt? I'd really like to be out there with ya'll. I'm tryin' to learn more ... and get more involved."

"Uhh ... well ... sure there, Reverend. You're always welcome with us." Bull replied, a little surprised and with just a slight hint of disappointment. Bull knew he'd now be responsible for the good Reverend, and it would be up to him to keep him safe. Reverend Arbuckle also invited himself to the Baptist Men's Group annual Christmas retreat at the Wampum Lodge, so by the time the January pheasant hunt came around, Reverend Arbuckle was ready to battle the birds, and become well acquainted with the men.

The day of the hunt, Bull kept up a pace to match Champ's, who was a good dog, a better dove and duck dog, but he held his own with the pheasant.

"Slow up a bit. Champ's got something." Bull whispered back to the men while focused on the spot Champ was pointing. We all lined up to shoot if a rooster flew.

"Easy now ... he's onta' one." Bull whispered.

"What's he on ...?" Reverend Arbuckle asked quietly.

The three of us held our gaze into the tall grass, silent and stoic. Arbuckle got the message. Just then, Champ's left paw lifted, and he leaned forward pushing his tail straight back. The moment lengthened. My heart beat filled my ears. Then WHAP, WHAP, WHAP, WHAP, the fast thumping of a pheasant's wings on the wind broke the silence, and the big rooster leapt from his cover and made a run for it. Bull tracked with his 12-gauge, but the bird turned suddenly and headed right for Reverend Arbuckle!

Arbuckle hollered, then flinched and hit the deck as the bird nearly took off his big orange hunting cap. "Is it gone yet? Jeez, that bird was AFTER ME! He *knew ya'll* were gonna kill him. How'd he know that?!"

Bull spun around already annoyed, "Shhhh. You're gonna spook the rest of the birds."

"There's *more*?!? Ya'll mean that's not the only one out here?"

"Now Reverend, you know damn well we didn't come out here for just one bird." Bull barked back.

Arbuckle, pursed his lips and shrugged his eyebrows, and mouthed *sorry*. "Clearly, I missed that detail, Bull."

We trudged on another five minutes till Champ dropped his tail, and Bull lowered his gun. "Well, whatever *was* out here has left. Let's pack it in and head back to the lodge. We'll go ahead and get dinner on for the rest of the men."

"Gosh, I'm really sorry. I've just never been strafed by a murderous pheasant before and I yelled. Gosh darn it, I just yelled. Sorry, I couldn't help it. I was startled."

Nodding as if to accept the apology, Bull Harlan marched on.

That evening we all gathered around the dinner table at the lodge. I was the only kid within 20 miles of the camp and felt honored to be there. The Baptist Men's

Group hunting party was a unique mix of old farts there to actually hunt, middle-aged insurance salesmen looking for a few new policies, and future sons-in-law pressed into a weekend of tribal interrogation. The old men used these weekends of escape to really cut loose. Nobody ever admitted to drinking, but Mr. Woolbuddy's "special" hot cider was consumed by the gallon. With every drop, the louder and taller the tales became around the campfire.

Warmed under a blanket of stars and stories, I watched as the glowing red and orange embers of the campfire carried the yarns straight up to the heavens. I'm sure, in some cultures, those embers were sought after, thought to deliver prayers, news and whatever else the living needed to send to the dead and the spirit world, but at the Baptist Men's Hunting Weekend, mostly the men did their best to avoid the flying sparks.

Several years back, some campfire embers found their way onto Randal Jenkins' hair piece and burned plum through it. Infused into the aroma of the heart pine wall paneling, the faint smell of burned hair and slow roasted Brylcreem still lingered in the lodge. So, tonight the men were extra careful not to get too close to the rising column of orange and red, especially Randal.

We sat outside till what must've been midnight, me cozied under my grandad's lucky hunting quilt, doing my best to soak up the knowledge that can only be learned around a camp fire. This was a special time, and I knew it.

The morning came early and we woke to the smell of sausage frying and coffee boiling. At the lodge, coffee was boiled, not brewed. The old red coffee pot had boiled thousands of gallons of dirty water, laden with the hopes of a happy hunt and residual tastes of the cheapest coffee grounds H-E-B sold. After the proper length of time, cold spring water was poured along the edge of the big pot which caused the bulk of the grounds to settle to the bottom. After a gentle pour, the red pot was returned to the fire until the next man stood ready with a cup.

The breakfast was hearty and the conversation nearly non-existent.

"Sleep well, Bull?" Mr. Woolbuddy asked.

"I did … coffee please, sir."

Already sipping on his first cup of instant coffee he must have made in his room, Reverend Arbuckle walked into the room wearing fuzzy pants, slippers, and a shirt that said "Hunting a Good Night's Sleep".

"Good morning, men. I didn't know ya'll were gonna be gettin' up so early." Arbuckle chirped.

Nobody answered him. They just kept sipping their coffee.

"Fine morning for a pheasant hunt, isn't it, Matt."

When a boy is asked a direct question, he has to answer. I put my orange juice down, smiled and said "Yes, sir, fine morning."

It was a fine morning, but Reverend Arbuckle's choice of clothing was just not what the men were expecting. No doubt, none of them would've been caught wearing any of the sorts.

After breakfast, we all loaded up our hunting vests with enough shells for the morning, along with enough to fight a top-secret CIA mission in South America should we be needed. We'd all tossed on an extra layer, because the blue norther had blown in after we went to bed and dropped the temp another 20 degrees. The wind was really whippin' up so it felt even colder.

"Alright, men, this mornin's gonna be a tough one out there. The birds are gonna be fast and our shootin' is gonna need to be tight to hit them, 'specially if the wind is in our face." Bull always said something pertinent before stepping out of the door.

Reverend Arbuckle, now dressed for hunting, emerged again into the main room. "Did I miss the speech? Well ... sorry. I hate missin' the speech, but let's say a quick prayer." Arbuckle wasn't an idiot. He might not have been a hunter nor had any sense of what manly men wore to breakfast on a hunt, but he knew nobody could argue over a prayer.

"Lord, help us to remember this morning, this hunt is truly about building your Kingdom on Earth. It's about fellowship and bolstering our fellow man, not belittling one another into a predetermined mold but helping each other blossom into the fullest existent of your perfect creation. And also, Lord, please don't let any of us get hurt, especially by a man-hatin' pheasant. In Jesus name we pray…amen."

We loaded up onto an old farm truck with a weathered stake bed. All of us fit, but just barely. Bouncing through the field, the men were quiet, likely still recovering from Mr. Woolbuddy's hot cider. As the wind stirred around my ears, I knew something was about to change in my life, but I wasn't sure what. When the truck came to a stop, Bull hopped out of the cab and dropped an old bucket that he turned upside down behind the bed for the older men to use while getting out.

"Watch your step," Bull said. "Now, Jim, when we get out there, put Matthew between us. Matt, the birds are gonna come quick, so shoot fast but remember only turn twenty degrees right or left. Okay? Don't want to shoot me or your dad."

"Yes, sir."

"On a day like today with the wind, it's real easy to turn too far and shoot someone standin' next to you."

"Yes sir. I'll remember. I won't shoot anyone."

Smiling at Bull, I took my place in the line abreast formation, and out we went, guns ready to fire if a bird popped up. Champ ran ahead with his nose sniffing everything in sight, bobbing along, darting back and forth in search of a wonder bird. Not long into the line, Champ flushed out a big hen, but nobody even flinched. Not even Arbuckle. The men just hollered "hen" and kept walking.

It was another ten minutes into the hunt before the first rooster was shot. By the end of the first field, we had three in bags. Things were really going well. Even Bull was happy. At the next field, there was a slight draw to the land so we started out going downhill before we worked our way up to the ridge line on top. As soon as we stepped out, two big roosters flew, going in opposite directions.

Boom, boom, boom, three shots were fired. Reverend Arbuckle and my dad each got one. Before long, Reverend Arbuckle looked like a hunter from one of those fancy hunting magazines. He had the pheasant stuffed into his vest in no time and a smile across his whole face.

There was an air of confidence among the Baptist Men's Group this morning but as we crested the ridge, that's when it happened. Just like a scene from a movie.

As we continued in our line abreast formation, Reverend Arbuckle vanished. Swooomump, was all I heard. When I turned around, he was just gone. Not even his bright orange hat could be seen. He just disappeared.

I whispered to my dad "Reverend Arbuckle's gone."

"Gone? Where'd he go?" Dad said.

Seeing as how I was the only person there with any hearing to mention, I said "I don't know, Dad, I just heard a swooomump noise and he was gone." When we walked back over our steps in the tall grass, but there wasn't a trace of Arbuckle. It was like he'd been raptured. He was just plain gone.

Dad tapped Bull on the shoulder "Arbuckle's gone."

"Gone? What the hell?" Bull whistled for Champ, and we all walked over to where he should've been. There was just high grass and no trace of Arbuckle. Bull waved for the truck and, as the driver approached, he hollered, "We're down a man."

"Down a man? Where'd he go?" asked the old rancher who drove the truck.

"Well, we have no clue, Matthew said he just heard a swooomump sound and he vanished."

"Hmm, well, he can't stay gone forever. Let's go have a look."

We crawled up onto the back of the truck so we could see farther. The old rancher eased the old truck down the ridge to the area where I last saw Reverend Arbuckle.

"You know, this hillside's where my grandparents' homestead was. Nothing left now but some old foundation stones," said the old rancher.

"Where was their well?" asked Bull with frustration in his tone.

"Don't know. My great grandpapy's been dead a long time. Never asked him, but I reckon they did have one. Never seen it, and I've been all over this land."

"Well … Baptist ministers don't just disappear." Bull chuckled.

As the wind blew, I heard something that sounded like the cry of a wounded rabbit. Even Mr. Jenkins noticed it.

"Over there! Hear that?" Mr. Jenkins shouted back to Bull.

"Yup…I hear it, too!" Bull said.

Before long, we all heard the high-pitched cry of something wounded, it was muffled, but it was certainly a crying animal. I jumped down out of the truck and started on foot.

Dad hollered out, "Careful, Matt. If he fell in something, don't get too close. We don't need you down there too."

I eased up toward the noise and crawled through the grass on my hands and knees. I moved about seven feet forward and pushed right through some thick thatch. Then I saw it. There was a big hole with lots of grass and thatch covering it like a web.

"Hey! There's a big hole here." I shouted to Dad.

Bull and the rest of the Baptist Men's Group jumped off the truck bringing some of the stakes from the truck bed with them. They pulled back the thatch and laid some of the boards down across the hole. Sure enough down in the bottom of what appeared to be the remains of a hand dug well sat Reverend Arbuckle.

Bull hollered down, "Arbuckle, you okay?"

In between the moans, Arbuckle ranted. "No! I'm NOT okay, I'm down here in this hole and I'm scaaaareeeed! Ya'll don't leave me down here. Get me out of here! Heeeelp! Help!"

"You're gonna have to shut up if you want our help," Bull barked back, his voice full of frustration. Bull was a lot of things, but he certainly wasn't the kind of man who was gonna let Reverend Arbuckle die down in a hole. Bull was also the kind of man to help Reverend Arbuckle keep what was left of his dignity. So, he had to shut him up before all the men gathered round.

"First, those damn fuzzy pants, now this," mumbled Bull quietly. He and the old rancher pulled some rope from behind the front seat. They backed the truck up to the edge of the hole and tied one end of the rope onto the bumper. On the other end of the rope, they fashioned a big loop for Reverend Arbuckle to wrap around his body.

"Okay, Arbuckle, we're gonna toss down this rope and you need to put it under your arms. You understand?"

"I think so. You gonna save me, Bull?"

"We're gonna try, but you're gonna have to help. When the truck starts pulling, you're gonna have to climb up and really use your legs. Like a rock climber. Bounce off the sides and help keep the rope free. Okay?"

The old rancher started up the farm truck and eased into low gear. He gave it lots of throttle and eased off the clutch. Errrrr, errr, errrrrr went the truck, as the rope moved up. It was working. I could see Arbuckle, still a bit groggy from likely hitting his head, putting his feet on the wall and rising up towards the edge.

"Keep it comin'," barked Bull.

Arbuckle seemed okay, but then—. he hollered. Well … it really wasn't a holler, it was more like a shriek. "OH - MY - GOD. IT'S GOT ME! IT'S GOT ME!" Arbuckle screamed in full blown panic.

Mr. Woolbuddy grabbed his flashlight and stuck it down between the boards to get a better look. Mr. Woolbuddy's face grimaced in horror.

"What the hell is it, Woolbuddy?" yelled Bull.

"Well, it appears that pheasant he shot has come back to life."

"The pheasant?"

"Yeah … that big ole' pheasant. Looks like it's sunk its claws into his hunting vest and it's just peckin' the hell out of his face. You might need to see this for yourself."

As Bull shone the light down the hole, the blood curdling screams got worse. The pheasant's blood-red eyes and Arbuckle's terror-filled moans were too much for my dad to tolerate.

"Matt, go back to the truck. You don't need to see this. We'll get him out."

Bull hollered down, "Damnit Arbuckle, just punch it!"

"I can't! Ya'll got to help me!" Followed by the intense plunking of what sounded like a blunt spoon plunging in and out of Jello in a wooden bowl. His speech was broken by the terrorizing pecks of the pheasant. "It's that——demon——bird———from yesterday! It was a trap—-a —— trap——oh——Lawd——-heeeeelpppp meeeeeeee!"

Arbuckle spouted his hate for the demon pheasant, like a redneck Shakespearian monologue. When his head crested the rim of the old well, Bull Harlan tore the pheasant from Arbuckle's chest and wrung its neck, then shot it point blank. The demon bird exploded like a dandelion blown at close range. The air was filled with the smell of gun powder and pheasant feathers.

Like a freshly landed catfish, Arbuckle laid there motionless. Bull rolled him over and just stared down at his freshly pecked, bloody face. "Well ... I've never seen anything like this. You really know how to spice up a hunt, Reverend."

Bull grabbed what was left of the tail of the pheasant and we all helped Reverend Arbuckle into the truck. Once we got the stakes back into the bed rails, we bounced our way to the cabin.

That afternoon, Mr. Woolbuddy patched up Reverend Arbuckle's face with some torn toilet paper, as if he were treating several hundred shaving cuts. He told Arbuckle to rest and not to worry about anything for the rest of the day.

When it came time for dinner, Arbuckle, who'd been asleep for some time, emerged from his room. His face was pocked with little blood-soaked toilet paper plugs, his left eye blackened and his right ear scratched. He walked out and just stood in the main room ... silent.

Bull stood up from his fireside chair, walked over, and extended his hand, never losing eye contact. "Glad you're alright, Arbuckle. You're one tough hombre."

Arbuckle burst into tears, "Oh … thank you, Bull. I just knew I was gonna die out there. You know what I mean. DIE. I thought I was gonna."

Bull pushed his hand over Reverend Arbuckle's mouth. "Shhhh. Just don't." Bull smiled. "Let's go have dinner."

That night around the campfire Arbuckle told us all how, when he fell into the hole, he whacked his head on a field stone and didn't remember anything until he saw Mr. Woolbuddy's flashlight. He thinks that's what woke up the demon bird.

"At first, I thought it was the light. You know … *THE* light. The *Jesus Light*, then I heard Bull and thought I don't think Jesus sounds like Bull Harlan … no offense Bull, but I still thought I was gonna die."

As the embers glowed and floated up towards heaven, the healing powers of the Holy Spirit and a great campfire went to work. By the time morning broke, all was made right, and the Baptists Men's Group hunting trip was another momentous success.

CHAPTER 2

FEBRUARY

THE RODEO

Every February, the entire Nation of Houston, and all of its surrounding kingdoms, take the month off and host the world's finest rodeo and exposition of Texan culture ever produced. Even the Ancient Egyptians would've marveled at this spectacle.

It takes place on the grounds of the 8th Wonder of the World, The Houston Astrodome, which in itself is worth traveling to see. Since its inception in 1932, Texans have been making pilgrimages to the Houston Livestock Show and Rodeo.

Even High Bluffians, who live on the edge of the earth, have a steady track record of attending. Every year, the only bus operation in High Bluff, Big Don's Executive Charters, drives up for all the important shows, offering door to door service between High Bluff and the rodeo entrance.

Big Don rolls out at 2:00 pm and pulls back into the H-E-B parking lot just after 2 am. It's a lot for one day, but it's also the only way someone from High Bluff can see a rodeo and Def Leppard in the same night.

For generations, Texans have clambered over the finely printed collector's program. Inside the program is the coveted schedule for not only the rodeo, but the after-rodeo music line up. Folks would go to blows to be the first with tickets for the big nights.

The time Elvis played the rodeo, there was almost an outright catastrophe down at the Country Kitchen's pay phone. Ms. Wanda LaFay was much younger back then and nearly knocked out Bull Harlan's front teeth while using the phone's receiver as a weapon to keep would-be takers away. She got two tickets for the show that day, but nobody wanted to go with her after seeing how she snapped.

The day tickets went on sale was always a quiet one around town. Rodeo goers seemed to be out sick from work, stores were never full, and Mr. Presley never cut hair, 'cause his bursitis was 'flairin' up somethin' awful.

Since Dad worked for the phone company, he knew the real story. It was one of the busiest days for General Telephone, the old electromechanical switches working overtime, clattering away making all the connections. These switches had replaced banks of operators years back but still weren't much more advanced than someone with a patch cable.

In the back of the building where all this took place, Dad and Mr. Fred, who worked with him, could hear the cacophony of voices all calling Houston. "Five for Willie Nelson, please." "What do you mean you're sold out!" "Well, thank you for the help. Would you like to go with me to the show *if* I can find some tickets? Well ... it was worth a shot 'cause you sure sound purdy."

Dad heard everything down there at work and often could piece things together pretty well as far as what was going around High Bluff. By the afternoon, Mr. Presley's bursitis was often better and folks were filing back into work and to the H-E-B.

During the days before the rodeo, folks with tickets often reconnected with old friends, boys got new girlfriends, and all sorts of things seemed to go right for the folks with "spares on hand". But the linchpin in the hierarchy of rodeo for High Bluffians was Big Don. If Big Don didn't like you, you weren't gettin' on the bus. And Big Don didn't like a lot of people, but he did like steak. So, he always seemed to have plenty of filet mignon come January.

Big Don had a master's degree in music but driving buses was more profitable. His wife, JoAnn, was the sweetest thing you'd ever met. She always rode in the back of the bus and served drinks along with her famous homemade snacks while Big Don tapped away the miles on the steering wheel to whatever song was playing in his head.

Riding on Big Don's bus was like flying first class, especially for High Bluff folks. When the time came to make the trips to Houston, folks turned out in their finest western duds. Starched Wrangler jeans, crisp white shirts and new Stetsons were the fashion of choice for men, and boots were a must. Ladies had all varieties of wears, but like the men, a stylish pair of boots and a fine hat were necessary before heading out. Big Don had a special rack in the bus's storage locker for all the hats. Each hat holder had a seat number and held the hat in place for the duration of the trip. It was much like transporting fine China, and Big Don knew it.

This year was an especially big year, because our very own Samuel N.C. Reynolds was riding bulls on opening night. (The N.C. stood for National Champion. His parents were hopeful.)

National's parents, Boone and Margarite, named him National Champion because Ms. Margarite said he bucked so hard in the womb, she knew he'd be a great bull rider, just like his father. Boone worked hard on an oil lease but rode bulls well into his 30's until he decided he was too broken to keep going. He'd made it to the PBR Finals himself, but never placed because of a serious injury his last year.

During the month of February, National was more famous than all the Wildcat Quarterbacks, and ate for free down at the Country Kitchen. He was given a hero's sendoff when he pulled away in his old Chevy. If High Bluff did one thing right, we could send off a champion—especially one named National Champion Reynolds.

Opening Saturday, we all gathered up as Big Don pulled into the parking lot.

"Afternoon, Don."

"Howdy, Bull, Ms. Juanita, ya'll are right up front. JoAnn's got some of her special bacon cheddar popovers hot and ready for ya."

Bull Harlan and Ms. Juanita settled in, and we all took our places. This year, Eugene and I were riding together just behind my parents, 'cause his parents couldn't go. We'd known each other since we were three and we were practically brothers. Eugene often reminded me that, even if my folks hadn't gone, going to the rodeo was a God-given right for Texans.

Kitty and Reverend Arbuckle even showed up for the trip.

"Arbuckle, nice boots." Bull said with a nod as they got on the bus.

"Well, thank you, Bull. I even picked them out."

"Well, of course you did, a man always picks out his own boots. Nice ones." Bull winked back as he cut into his popover with his pocket knife.

In a few short minutes, we were off to Houston. The whole Reynolds family was driving up behind us in a long caravan of pickup trucks, minivans and a few borrowed church vans over-stuffed with kids, cousins and honorary Aunts and Uncles to help them stay fed and entertained.

As the sun set at our backs, the stars shined bright with opportunity for National. This was his big chance and we all wanted to be there with him, and seeing George Strait was a great bonus. Ms. Wanda LaFay led us all in song from her seat near the back of the bus as we neared the Astrodome.

"The Stars at night are big and bright" she sang as we all clapped the next part and sang out "Deep in the heart of Texas!"

I always loved these road trips with Big Don, and so did Eugene because Ms. JoAnn served us so much hot chocolate, we were sugar-fueled like two humming birds ready to fly across the ocean. We bounced off the bus and right into the rodeo.

As far as the eye could see, it was lights. Carnival rides, the midway, the

BBQ cookoff, and, yes, the Astrodome! Lit up like a giant round mountain, it was filled with Texans and want-to-be Texans from all over the globe. We all split up and went our separate ways inside, because our seats were scattered all over the place.

Eugene and I got some food before we caught up with my mom and dad and took our seats. Gnawin' on my jalapeño corndog, I watched the lights inside the Astrodome go dark.

Thousands of little sparkling things bounced across the domed roof and all of sudden, a lone white horse with the rodeo queen in the saddle appeared at the center of the arena, lit with a single spotlight. She glittered and sparkled so brightly I almost needed to squint. In her hand was a large, stately mahogany pole and there, draped from just beneath the brass eagle on top, was the star-spangled banner.

We all stood up and removed our hats. The National Anthem played, and just as it ended, the lights all came on and the opening rodeo parade appeared. Over the years, past US Presidents, Governors and hundreds of other dignitaries and important people have ridden in the opening parade atop longhorn steers, old wagons and the backs of pickup trucks. This very evening, marching bands filled the air with music and the spotlights danced as the announcer called out all the names of the big wigs.

The opening pomp was on par with any royal event, only no gowns or capes, but there were plenty of crowns on top of cowboy hats and beauty contests sashes … lots of sashes.

When the parade ended, the announcer invited everyone to take their seats for the start of the rodeo. The night wore on with lots of big moments, but the one we'd all come to see was happening at the end—the bull riding. A few corn dogs later, it was time.

We all watched National get into the chute. He'd drawn a bull named Guerrero, which means warlike in Spanish. Solid black with dark brown eyes, the bull had a nasty mangled hump and sharp curved horns that looked like ones right off the head of Satan.

The cowboys gathered around behind National, and whacked him on the back for good luck. He sat down on Guerrero. Right away, the bull kicked and bounced in the chute and the cowboys worked to help National settle in. Even the announcers talked about how mean Guerrero appeared to be.

Reverend Arbuckle and Kitty were two rows in front of us, and he looked back towards Dad. "Think he's okay?"

"He's gotta ride him either way." Dad said.

Before Arbuckle could turn his head, the chute swung open and the place went nuts! National hung on in perfect form, and we all watched as the clock counted up towards eight. The buzzer rang and before we knew it, National claimed a perfect ride!

Holy smokes! We all jumped up with excitement as National bailed off Guerreo. The bull had taken an awkward path so

National jumped off just about the middle of the arena. The clowns had done their best to keep up, but when Guerreo turned around, National was all alone. Guerreo charged straight for him as one of the bull fighters dove forward to try and turn his path. Guerreo picked him up just like a fork lift and, still at full speed, crashed into National throwing him and the bull fighter into the metal fencing around the edge of the arena. They both just laid there.

Guerreo kicked dust–mad and ready to charge again. By this point, the other bull fighters and clowns circled the two men, and more clowns and fighters attracted Guerreo's attention. It was the most heroic thing I'd ever seen. Reverend Arbuckle ran down towards National, and by the time he got there, the clowns were loading him onto a stretcher.

I don't even remember what happened next, but, in a daze, we all walked back down to the entrance of the rodeo to where Big Don was waiting. Somehow, he'd gotten word about National, so we all loaded up and headed to the hospital to wait for news. I don't think anyone talked as we sped over to the Medical Center, but I do remember the ladies praying. Reverend Arbuckle was already there, because he rode in the ambulance with Ms. Margarite.

When we pulled up, Kitty came forward. "Don, let me go inside, I'll see what's happening." About an hour later, Kitty emerged with Reverend Arbuckle.

"I don't know much, but I can tell you this, National is alive, but his back is broken and so are his hip and arms." Reverend Arbuckle fought back tears. "Our National was saved by those brave men down there, I'll never think of a rodeo clown again as just someone dressed up funny. Those men are *heroes*. I've just never seen anything like it, and tonight, one of those brave men is laying up there beside our National 'cause he was trying to save him. It's just … it's just the most *heroic thing*."

He and Kitty took their seats. He wiped away his tears, mumbling "I've just never … never seen anything like that. I had *no* idea." We all knew Reverend Arbuckle could get worked up during a sermon or over some special music, but we'd never seen him like this.

Eugene and I fell asleep almost immediately 'cause it was late, real late, especially by the time we left. It was always a quiet drive home, but tonight, it was especially quiet because rather than talking, everyone was praying. Praying for National, but also thanking God for those brave men who remind us life is a balancing act with risk.

At the rodeo, this is always driven home when someone gets hurt, but I've never seen a cowboy *not* ride when the next bull is ready.

CHAPTER 3

MARCH

THE TRASH CANNON

Jude Williams's Uncle Joel lived outside town on a caliche road, just past the Cotton Blossom. Which was convenient for Uncle Joel, since he was always there if DT had it open. To say Uncle Joel was a heavy drinker would be unfair to real drinkers. Uncle Joel drank, but it wasn't something he was known for. It was just something he did, much like breathing.

His old trailer house sat on a few acres of land he'd bought when he came home from Vietnam. He worked around town doing odd jobs but mostly he helped DT around the Cotton Blossom, doing handy work that didn't involve anything real regular or dependable.

In small towns, folks know just about everything going on with everyone, and High Bluff was no different, but that helps, especially when you're someone like Uncle Joel. He'd served in the Army and served valiantly, but when he came home, the sadness of what he'd seen over there was just too much, so he kept it numbed up under a river of whiskey and laughter.

Everyone knew Uncle Joel, and everyone accepted Uncle Joel so he contributed where he could, and when he couldn't, we all understood it was because he'd already given so much. Years ago, the Army showed up and presented him with a box of ribbons and metals that somehow were never awarded to him when he left the Army. Uncle Joe never spoke of it, but we all knew.

On Sundays, Jude would drive out and take a proper Sunday dinner to Uncle Joel. They'd sit outside and laugh the afternoon away with stories from the week or about anything they thought was funny. Jude would also help him out if there was anything around his trailer that needed helping with.

On this particular Sunday, Uncle Joel mentioned he needed some help with a large pile of trash. "Jude, we just need to move all this stuff down to the old well, then we'll have some fun."

"What's in all these bags anyways?" asked Jude.

"Just some old junk DT asked me to haul away from the Blossom earlier in the week. Mostly old junk from the back store room."

"Hmm … anything worth keepin'?"

"Not a damn thing, it's just old crap. Paint cans, some old paint rollers and a whole bunch of old pickle jars and junk like that."

"Huh. Wonder why he's been holdin' on to it all these years?"

"If I knew why DT did half the stuff he did, I'd be runnin' the Cotton Blossom myself!" Uncle Joel said, breaking out into a smoker's cough-filled laugh.

As Uncle Joel took in a nice long drag, his Marlboro Red struck a perfect balance between ash and filter. It hung there in harmony, propped up by the South Texas wind. "Once we get all this junk down the hole, I'll light it off and let it burn down." he said with a wink as he let the ash drop.

"What is the old hole anyway?" Jude asked.

"When I moved in, lady said it was an old hand-dug well, but it's been dry for 20 years or more. Nothing but dust and old junk, so I just keep addin' to it, burn it down every few months, then fill it back again. I call it, my burnin' well." Uncle Joel kept on laughing and smoking as they worked to push the bags of DT's old junk down the hole.

From inside Uncle Joel's trailer, the smell of beans and ham simmering' down found their way outside. Jude had brought over his old slow cooker and that smell somehow made it feel more like a home. Tonight, he and Joel would be dining in high style, complete with jalapeño corn bread Jude had made earlier in the day.

Ever since Brandy ran off with that roughneck from Houston, Jude had to cook every night for his little daughter, Stormy, and himself. But Sunday afternoons were reserved for Uncle Joel, so Jude's mom would come over and make sure Stormy was tended to. These were special nights for all involved but especially Uncle Joel.

That evening, as the sun went down, Jude and Uncle Joel pulled some old camp chairs around the burnin' well and settled in for a night out under the stars. Cold beer and hot trash, finished off with hammy beans and fixins'. This was fine livin'.

As Uncle Joel was gettin' ready to light off the trash fire, Jude ran back into the trailer to grab two fresh beers. As Jude jogged back, he watched Uncle Joel dump a whole five gallon can of diesel fuel, and whatever old oil he'd had stored up behind his shed on top of the trash.

Jude laughed to himself, cause that old oil can must have held several gallons, seeing's how they'd just changed the oil in both their trucks last weekend.

When Jude got back to the fire pit, Uncle Joel held up a match and said "You have the honors tonight."

"Oh, no. I saw all that junk you tossed in while you thought I wasn't lookin'. It's all you tonight!"

"Ya big sissy, come on and light her off!"

"No way! I need my eyebrows and hair. Gotta look good if I'm ever gonna get a new woman."

"Ain't no women gonna be interested in ya' if you can't live a little. Light the damn match!"

Jude gave in and lit a match. Tossing it in, it went out when it hit the oil.

"Here, try again. But hold it down there on that old paper bag to the left. She'll light then."

Jude knew better than to take Joel's advice, but since the beer was workin' on him, he lit the match and carefully held it on the bag like Uncle Joel suggested. Nothing. It blew right out. "Here, Uncle Joel, you're gonna' have to show me how it's done."

Uncle Joel walked back to his shed and fashioned up an old Dr. Pepper bottle with a big long fuse made out of cotton rope. He soaked the rope in some more diesel fuel and then filled the bottle with more diesel, too. Uncle Joel lit the rope with his Zippo and then ran back towards the burnin' well hollerin' like a wild man. He chucked the flaming Dr. Pepper bottle into the well.

It bounced a bit going down and then somehow slipped between the bags of trash and disappeared. It was a rather dramatic moment, followed by a thin finger of smoke rising up from between the old paper bags along with the gentle sound of flickering flames.

Relieved, Jude smiled. "There. Sounds like it lit. Now we just wait and enjoy it." Jude said.

"Hell nah! We need some flames up here to help keep us warm. Stand by, I'm callin' in another air strike."

While Uncle Joel fixed up the next Dr. Pepper bottle, Jude decided he'd dash in the trailer and check on dinner. "You call in yer' air strike, I'll make sure the pilot's food's okay."

"Copy all!" Uncle Joel said with his arms spread out like a jet fighter, running back towards his shed for another load of diesel.

Jude scooped out Uncle Joel's share of hammy beans, but even though it'd been simmering in the slow cooker, it wasn't quite hot enough. He decided he'd nuke it in the old family microwave. It had belonged to Jude's mom when he was a kid. He set the old mechanical timer on it and waited for the familiar sound of the bell. That ding would always take him back to when he was kid, waitin' on his mom to warm up his milk at bed time, or zappin' his oatmeal on a cold morning.

Jude's mom was Uncle Joel's sister and she loved him dearly and was also happy when Jude went over to spend time with him. Family pictures smothered Uncle Joel's refrigerator. Nearly everybody was on that fridge, but you couldn't help but notice all the ones of Joel and Jude. He had a crudely written, handmade sign over the section of picture with Jude and him. "My Nephew Jude" stood in giant handwritten letters atop the power company magnet that held it and about fifteen other pictures to the fridge door.

Ding went the microwave and Jude snapped back from reminiscing.

As Jude swapped out the bowls, he heard what sounded like bottle rockets and just laughed to himself. "Ain't no tellin' what he's thrown down there now. Crazy Uncle Joel." Jude chuckled glancing back at the pictures.

This time, just before the ding, he clearly heard what sounded like a howitzer blast. Shhhuuuuuuuuuuump! Boooooom!! The whole trailer shook from the blast and over it all was the sound of Uncle Joel's "Yeeeeee-haaaaaw!!!!"

"Hooooh MY GAWD! Will ya' look at that! My GAWD, JUDE you ain't gonna believe THIS!" Uncle Joel shouted. "COME QUICK JUDE, it's prolly gonna blow again!"

Running out the trailer, Jude couldn't believe what he was seeing. A giant glowing rocket launch-shaped cloud of red, orange and yellow fiery embers arched up from the burnin' well and stretched out towards to western heavens.

Uncle Joel stood below it, hands on his hips, mouth slack jawed and grinning. "My Gawd Joel, can ya' believe it! Holy Hell man, check this out! I think it's bout' to blow again! Gawd, I just can't…."

Shhhhhhhhhuuuump! BOOOOOM! BOOOOOM! The burnin' well shot out a double belch, this time sending tiny burning debris even farther into the black night sky.

"Whooohoooo! Holy Hell, Jude! Ain't nobody gonna believe this!"

BOOOM! BOOOM! BOOOOM! Again, the burnin' well belched and shot debris flaming into the star covered sky. Jude starting to relax a bit, couldn't help but be mesmerized by the spectacle of it all. There was nothing around but scrub brush so even if it caught fire, it wouldn't spread past Uncle Joel's dirt patch.

Shhhhhhhuuuump! Boom! Boom! The well shot fire, hurling sparks—and Uncle Joe's old Army hat—into the night.

"Whoohoo! Holy Hell, Jude! Nobody's gonna believe this!"

"I thought that was just junk from the Cotton Blossom—you put your Army stuff down there, too?"

Joe's eyes stayed on the flames. "Yeah… let it burn." He exhaled slow, the kind of breath that carried years away with it.

The giant glowing ember horn stretched over two hundred feet. The smells of burnt oil and diesel fuel mixed with old tires, paint and God only knows what else had been shoved down the burnin' well over the years was all coming up now in a display of glorious redneck wondery.

It was the most incredible thing Uncle Joel had ever pulled off and *without even tryin'* thought Jude. Jude grabbed a fresh cold beer from the cooler and cracked it open for his Uncle Joel. "Here, you deserve this. This is the finest trash cannon I've ever laid eyes on!"

"Well, thank ya', I'm just glad yer' here to see it 'cause I haven't seen this kinda crap go down since 'Nam." Uncle Joel said with his arm stretched over Jude's shoulders hugging him.

"Hey at least these ain't real bullets!" Jude said.

"Well, ya' bring up a good point. I don't know 'cause there's some old shells down there too, prolly." Uncle Joel, broke into his smoker's laugh again and rinsed down the dust in his throat with a swig of beer. "Jude, this is just about the finest night I've had … maybe ever. I just can't believe this damn thing."

Shhhhhhuuuuuuummmm. BOOOM! BOOM! The burnin' well went off every ten minutes or so, and every time, Uncle Joel would howl at the moon and holler something out that only he understood.

That night, Jude and Uncle Joel fell asleep beside the trash cannon and slept right there til the cooing of the mourning doves woke them up. Grinnin' still from the night before amidst the dancin' smoke from the burnin' well, Uncle Joel laid back in his chair. "Suuuum night. Gawlee." Uncle Joel said raising his eyebrows up and down. "Looks like a fresh snow out here."

Jude's eyes strained out to the dirt patch and sure enough, ash and burned trash littered the whole area, like fresh virgin snow on a mountain top. The acrid smell of its unknown origin burned into the backs of their throats and helped lock in the memory forever.

"Sure does, Uncle Joel. How 'bout some coffee?" Jude smiled. "You just sit here and enjoy the moment. I'll go start a pot."

As Jude walked away, Uncle Joel, whispered to him. "Love ya' boy."

"I love you, too, Uncle Joel… Suuum night."

CHAPTER 4

APRIL

UNCLE CHARLIE'S RED CANOE

Uncle Charlie was my grandfather's best friend. He wasn't related by blood, but he was family none the less. Charlie and Red Campbell were inseparable as boys, and their brotherhood survived the gale force of the Great Depression, World War II and countless other storms, even a tragic family life.

Charlie's dad died at an early age, and Red's father died when he was a young teenager. Both boys became men early in life, and when war broke out, they both signed up right away. Charlie was selected for pilot training, but it turns out buzzing farmers' fields, and doing spins above ladies tending their clotheslines is the kind of stuff the Army Air Corps didn't take kindly to.

Charlie eventually became a radio operator on B-17's and flew a full set of missions in Europe. Enough to come home, but he volunteered for more. Red became a Marine aircraft mechanic and along the way earned a sharp shooter badge and eventually became a tail gunner on SBD dive bombers. He went to Midway, The Coral Sea, and many other dangerous, dusty strips in the Pacific.

Both men survived the war and settled down in Corpus Christi, just across the bridge from High Bluff. They'd traded Salado Creek for Corpus Christi Bay and Lake Mathis, but their lifelong passion for everything outdoors never waned. Red enjoyed fishing, but he really loved to hunt. Charlie enjoyed hunting, but he really loved to fish. So, Charlie usually had a boat and Red kept a deer lease. It was brotherly love at its best for Red and Charlie.

When I was coming up and old enough to remember, Charlie bought a little red Styrofoam canoe as a Christmas present for himself. He wanted one because during the winter, it was too cold for his preferred method of stalking trophy trout—wade fishing. The little red canoe was lightweight and perfect for hauling on top of his VW Bug down to Bird Island for an afternoon of chasing lunkers in the Laguna Madre. He'd paddle down onto the flats, catch a few big ones then head home.

As the winter continued, Uncle Charlie's love affair with his little red canoe deepened. It was big enough for two, but he only went on solo missions. This particular afternoon, he was especially excited because his brand-new Abu Garcia rod and reel combo had arrived, along with his newly stocked tackle box, filled with his secret weapon—Bass Assassin Sea Chad, the model with the chartreuse tail, silver belly and black sparkles on top.

When he drove the VW with the canoe on top, it looked like a brightly colored cartoon car. His tropical blue bug with the fire engine red canoe on top, laced down with electric yellow rope tied from both bumpers to the bow and stern, zooming down the road soaked in the symphony of the VW's whirling engine.

This particular afternoon, the water was flat and the wind was completely still which was rare for a spring day. It was still cool, but spring time in South Texas can be unpredictable as the cold fronts become less regular. He paddled out towards a big flock of seagulls feeding on the bait fish schooled below. This time of year, fishing under the birds is as good as it gets.

Anglers look out onto the horizon and spot a flock, but the absolute most certain sign of successful fishing is finding an oily looking, rainbow-colored film floating on top of the water. The big trout create this as they munch on their meals down below.

Uncle Charlie tossed his anchor and let out enough rope so he could fish in the spot by the big slick. He cast out a shiny new Bass Assassin tied to the end of his brand new and already beloved Abu Garcia combo rod and reel.

Ziiiiiing … plop. Direct hit! The Bass Assassin landed just the other side of the slick. He slowly wiggled and reeled in his lure, creating an almost perfect re-creation of a wounded bait fish. Within a few seconds, Uncle Charlie had a whopper pulling on his lure.

He reared back on the Abu Garcia and set the hook deep. The trout pulled so hard it dragged the tiny lead anchor weight. Uncle Charlie hollered with delight.

"Whoooooooeeeeeee! Red ain't gonna believe this! HA-HA! JACKPOT!" Uncle Charlie pulled the big trout out with his net, his heart racing. "32 inches!" The fish flopped into the cooler and kept thrashing about.

Charlie thought, *One more time*. He cast his line and, for the next thirty minutes, Uncle Charlie caught one whopper after the next. Nothing as big as the beast in the cooler, but, boy, was he having fun. He landed two more towards the end of the run, one 26 inches another 28 inches. This was shaping up to be the best day he'd ever had on the water.

One more cast. Just as the Bass Assassin hit the water, Uncle Charlie felt some water hit his neck. "Hmmm … what the heck?" He said out loud. He turned around and behind him, the sky was dark, dark black with little wispy stark white steam rolling off like the whole sky had just been paved over with hot asphalt. Moving across the mirror-still water, a white line of angry rain fell full of hate less than a mile away.

"Dag nabit! Where the heck did that come from!" Charlie reeled in the Bass Assassin and pulled up his anchor. He was at least a thirty-minute paddle back to Bird Island, and there was no way he'd make it. So, Uncle Charlie paddled over to a nearby spoil island. These tiny islands dot the flats and areas around the Intercostal Waterway all the way down the Laguna Madre. Just as Uncle Charlie got to shore and pulled the little red canoe onto the sand, the gust front hit the shoreline.

The wind whipped up to well over 40 knots, picking up the little red canoe like a grocery bag on a string. Uncle Charlie held on to the anchor rope, trying to pull it back down to earth, the little red canoe twisting and whipping around now over 10 feet in the air. The wind beat against Uncle Charlie's back, but he pulled the canoe back down, inch by inch. Getting back down, Uncle Charlie crawled inside it and set down.

"You're gonna have to do better than that storm! HA! Ain't takin' my canoe!"

Just as he finished his taunt, the big storm let out a bolt of lightning so big it splintered off into 5 forks. Shhhheeeekkk! BOOM! The thunder clapped so hard Uncle Charlie rolled out of the canoe and laid flat against the beach. In between the lightning strikes, Uncle Charlie tried to dig himself into the sand as to not be the tallest lump on the island.

The wind and rain continued to beat against him like a flock of angry pecking chickens that seemed to have more friends showing up by the second to peck right along with them. He pulled down his hat and laid as still as he could, only breathing in between lightning strikes. All around him, he could feel the reverberations from the wind and thunder between every gust and strike. It was a fury he'd never seen before from Mother Nature, not even in a hurricane. Hurricanes are big and powerful, but they're constant—angry but constant. This storm was irrational and violent, like a belligerent drunk, punching and causing harm to anything it could see or touch.

After a solid ten minutes, the worst passed and the wind and rain let up. When Uncle Charlie shook loose from the sand, his little red canoe was there beside him, well, half of it. The other half of the canoe came to rest about 100 yards away in the tall reed grass of the spoil island. When it was safe, Uncle Charlie walked over and retrieved it. He's a resourceful man, but not even Uncle Charlie could fix this. So, Uncle Charlie just sat back down in the sand and, waiting for the storm to move on, he plotted his escape.

Before long the angry storm that had torn apart his little red canoe moved out into the Gulf of Mexico. Uncle Charlie could see boats heading back down the Intercostal, presumably back to Bird Island. He tried signaling to some with a tiny mirror he kept in his tackle box, but none of them stopped. After an hour or so, he'd had enough.

He wrote a note to any would-be rescuers and said he was going to paddle along the shoreline or walk if he had to, but he was headed back to Bird Island. He grabbed his paddle, tackle box, and beloved Abu Garcia then knelt down in the longer half of the little red canoe and started paddling back to his VW Beetle.

He'd been underway no more than ten minutes when the unmistakable sound of a Coast Guard Helicopter grew close. Turning around, a bright white search light hit him squarely in the face. Like a driver getting pulled over by the police, Charlie paddled the 30 feet to the shore of North Padre Island and pulled what was left of his little red canoe onto the sand.

As the helicopter flew closer, the door on the side opened up, and a rescue swimmer appeared. A loud voice boomed down over the noise of the rotor wash from a big speaker on the bottom of the flying machine. "This is the United States Coast Guard, we're coming down to help." Looking up, Uncle Charlie wasn't sure what to do or say, so he just gave them a thumbs up.

The helicopter moved closer towards the shore. Sand and a fine mist from the water kicked up and blasted Uncle Charlie so badly he turned away and knelt down, pulling his hat over his face and eyes. The rescue swimmer called out, still swinging from the rope, "Don't worry, I'm coming over to you!" Again, Uncle Charlie just gave a thumbs up.

Once on the ground, the rescue swimmer ran down the beach and tapped Uncle Charlie on the shoulder. "Are you okay to walk?"

"Walk? Yeah, I'm fine. In fact, ya'll just leave me be, I'm fine to walk the rest of the way if that'd make you happier."

"No, sir, not a problem. Just hold on to me, and we'll get back safely. There's more bad weather moving in! A boater saw your distress call. We're here now. Let us help you."

Charlie reluctantly agreed, seeing how they were already here and all.

"I'll be right with you. just let me gather my things." Uncle Charlie darted off against the rotor wash and picked up his Abu Garcia rod and reel combo and his tackle box and ran back.

"Can't take anything, sir, you'll have to leave that stuff behind. I can only take you."

"Son, it's just a fishing rod and reel and … well, my tackle box."

"I know sir, but you'll have to leave them behind."

"Well, I've waited a long time for this one. You do know this is an Abu Garcia combo rod *and* reel? I'll just keep hold of it like this. We'll be fine."

"Yes, sir, I do know what that is. But it ain't going. Now just leave it over there and hold on, we've got to get going. Several more rescues to get to."

"I've survived WWII, and now you're telling me I've got to abandon my Abu Garcia 'cause some *communist* in Washington says I can't be rescued with it? *BASTARDS!*"

Uncle Charlie held on to the basket they sent down for him like the rescue swimmer instructed and was reluctantly hoisted into the helicopter. Before long the rescue swimmer was back inside and closed the door. As they zoomed away back to the Coast Guard station, Uncle Charlie watched his tackle box and Abu Garcia until he couldn't see them anymore.

"Sir, it's just the rules, but I'm glad you're alright. There's another line of weather moving in, so coming with us was the right choice."

"Communist bastards." Uncle Charlie slowly mouthed to the young man. "They've never had to abandon an Abu

Garcia." Looking at the rescue swimmer's hint at a smile, Charlie finally relented. "I know you're right, son, but it doesn't make it any easier. Thank you for the ride."

Uncle Charlie called Red to pick him up down at the Coast Guard station, and, before long, our phone rang at home. I can still hear Charlie and Dad talking.

"Jim, I need you take me down to the backside of Padre to pick up some stuff."

"Well … Hello to you, too, Charlie. What kind of stuff?" Dad asked.

"My Abu Garcia combo and tackle box. It's filled with brand new Bass Assassins and what's left of my canoe and a whole passel of fish. Can you help an old man in need out?"

"Sure, Charlie, we can go tomorrow morning."

"Now listen, Jim, I've got a big Q-beam spotlight if tonight would be better."

"Charlie, I ain't gettin' the boat out tonight. It's almost 9 o'clock, and more weather's due in." Dad hung up the phone and turned to me. "Get ready for a rescue mission in the morning. We've got to go get Charlie's canoe and tackle box."

Before sun up, we launched the boat and Uncle Charlie and Red were there to meet us at Bird Island. The Marine and the Airman boarded the boat with ropes and all kinds stuff appropriate for a rescue mission, coffee and tacos included.

As we motored down the backside of the island, I couldn't help but laugh to myself a bit. The thought of Uncle Charlie getting rescued by the Coast Guard, and complaining the whole time about leaving his rod and reel was funny, even to a twelve-year-old boy. Before long, we'd rescued his beloved Abu Garcia combo and his tackle box, along with half of the canoe.

"Hey, Jim, mind fetching the other half of the canoe? It's up yonder at that next spoil island."

Dad turned the boat into the wind and set a course for the little spoil island just over from where Uncle Charlie rode out the storm. We got it strapped down, and even found the ice chest with his fish, still on ice.

Aside from the canoe, Uncle Charlie's big adventure was turning out alright. By the time we got back to the dock, Red and Charlie had worked out a plan for repairing the little red canoe. It was a solid plan, and, as I write this now, I can attest it was successful, but that little red canoe was simply destined for disaster. Some things in life are just cursed, and that little red canoe was one of them.

Charlie and Red fiberglassed the whole thing and for several summers us kids would use it up at Lake Mathis. When we'd get out, our arms would be filled with itchy and sharp strands of fiberglass. At this point in its life, the damn thing had more in common with a cactus than a canoe. At some point, the paint faded so badly we thought maybe a coat of fresh red would cure not only its bad looks but cactus-like qualities.

That summer, my cousins and I painted the whole canoe with some red paint from the Lagarto Store just down from the lake house. The canoe looked great, but right after we launched for our inaugural paddle down the cove, the canoe started taking on water. Lots of water!

Turns out the paint we'd come into wasn't the best for the Styrofoam. The chemicals in the paint melted the foam under the prickly fiberglass, like an ice cream cone in the sun. Before long, the locust-like shell, now perfectly painted red, slowly sank to the bottom of Lake Mathis.

Truth be told, I wasn't sad to see it go. Cousin Marcus was a champion swimmer and I could dog paddle just fine, so we didn't even need rescuing. As for the canoe, it was going to be just fine on the bottom of the lake … where it likely belonged all along.

CHAPTER 5

MAY

THE RIVER TRIP

Blake Ellis is that friend, and we all have *that* friend. *That* friend is one of the most exciting things in your life, because they always seem to find trouble, even in the simplest and purest of things. Blake Ellis could not only find trouble, he relished in its discovery. Like a hippo in the wild staring into the sun on one of those Wild Kingdom videos they showed us in school, when trouble found Black Ellis, he'd raise his head and a glowing shine would erupt from his face with the found opportunity for havoc and potential mayhem. He was made for it!

Take fishing for instance. When we were just old enough to drive, Blake called and said "Hey, let's go up to the river and fish tomorrow night." His folks had a cabin along the Nueces River just north of High Bluff, but it had been a while since their last visit.

Blake's dad, Big Jim, built the cabin by hand. It wasn't anything to look at, just a cobbled together river shanty with a dock out back. Big Jim wasn't into building mansions, he was into building memories. Big Jim had fallen ill several years back, and the trips to the cabin were increasingly rare, so when Blake asked if he and I could stay the night and do some fishing, Big Jim agreed.

We drove up Friday night in Blake's old truck, and it didn't even break down along the way, which should have been enough foreshadowing for us to just turn around and drive back, but we pressed on.

Being two teenage boys, the thought of stopping for food and provisions never crossed our minds, so we just went straight to the cabin.

"Jeez … it's been a while since we've been here, Matt. It sure is grown up."

"Still looks the same though. I mean let's be honest, if it looked nice, Big Jim would hate it."

We both had a laugh then pulled out our flashlights to see how bad the inside was. This wasn't the kind of place that had a door knob. It had a big ole padlock on the front door and giant wooden handle to push open. Once inside, our flashlights knocked down a few cobwebs, but overall, it wasn't that bad. The old place was solid. It looked like hell, but it was dry and only drafty in places where it actually felt good. We opened up a few windows and let it air out a bit while we got the fire pit out back going.

That night, Blake and I sat outside and got our fishing tackle ready to attack the river monsters the next morning. It was a perfect late spring evening, clear sky, light breeze, and a new moon. This meant great fishing 'cause they wouldn't have been feeding at night.

Before first light, we hauled our stuff down to the dock but when we got there, the boat wasn't where it usually was. It was way too early to call Big Jim, so we just fished right there off the dock. Blake hooked into a massive catfish and hauled it up after a good fight. Seeing's how we hadn't eaten anything since before driving up, we fried the catfish up for breakfast and ate as the sun sauntered up past the horizon. Fed and watered, Blake noticed their boat was down at the neighbor's dock.

"There it is! I guess Dad got the neighbor to clean it up before we got here. Man, that was nice of him. Hard to believe, but I guess anything's possible. His gettin' sick sure has changed him, sometimes like this though, you know ... for the better." Blake said, while smacking on his last piece of catfish.

After cleaning up, we traipsed down to the neighbor's dock and felt around for the key under the center console. Sure enough, the key was right there on top of the gas tank. The tank was completely full too! I couldn't believe it. The neighbor had even stocked the old boat with fresh trot lines and new floaty jugs.

"Dude, check this out! There's enough soap blocks down here for all weekend! I can't believe Dad set this up for us."

Big Jim was a fair man, but he didn't tolerate any horse hockey. He'd been a pilot for Trans Texas, better known as Texas Tree Top Airways back in the day, flying old WWII surplus DC-3's but retired early when he punched the CEO. Back when Tree Top merged with a fancy jet company, the pilots got dealt a nasty deal. Big Jim wasn't afraid to speak up — even with his fist. He was a legend, a man of principal, and a man with a mean right jab. Just ask that airline President.

Big Jim must have truly appreciated our interest in the old place and had their old boat cleaned up so maybe we'd want to go back and help keep the cabin up? That's all we could figure.

Blake and I fired up the old Evinrude and motored down river towards the big bend. We baited the trot line hooks with the lye soap and set the rest of the lines on the opposite side of the big bend in the river then headed on back to the cabin.

For a Saturday morning, the river was completely quiet. Nobody was up there. We docked the old boat back at the cabin and tied it off just like old times. We figured it was high time to go buy some groceries and maybe a few lightbulbs for the outside, so we loaded up and rode into George West.

George West is a tiny town, the kind with more cattle than people and slim pickins for grocery stores. We wrangled up some eggs, milk and more cornmeal for frying catfish and even found some lightbulbs. There was a small taqueria down from the grocer that had something on the grill that smelled too good to pass up. Blake pulled over and our noses led us right up to the order window. We left with a bag of hot tortillas and enough breakfast tacos to hold us over till we had some fish.

Our short trip turned into a 2-hour ordeal, but that was okay. We'd gotten everything we'd set out for. Pulling back up to the cabin, there were noticeably more trucks and cars on the road. Even the neighbor's house had a shiny new Corvette out front. Now this was something. Corvettes are not the usual suspects on dirt roads next to river shanties, but there was sure enough one next door. As we unloaded, the old man across the street was doing the same thing.

"Ain't seen ya'll in a while! Glad yer' back, Blake."

"Yes, sir, we're gonna stay the night, but we'll be back again soon. Say, who's the new neighbor down there with the blue Vette?"

"Oh ... I don't know his name, they're *real* new. He's their son, big grown fella ... built like an ox. Ha! Jenkins. I think is their family name."

We started haulin' in our supplies and opening up the windows again when we heard the Jenkin's guy start hollerin'.

"YEAH BABY! Gonna be a good day down here! Mötley Crüe on the radio!" He started blastin' the stereo inside the old cabin so loud it was a wonder the walls didn't fall over.

We no sooner heard the neighbor holler than the old phone hanging in the kitchen rang. Blake and me both jumped, 'cause hearin' a phone out here doesn't happen much. It was Big Jim.

"Hey, Dad, we just got back. Ran into town and bought some light bulbs and we're gonna spend the afternoon gettin' everything in shape up here. Listen, we sure appreciate you gettin' the old boat in shape for us. That new neighbor guy even loaded it up with trot lines and fresh lye soap."

"Blake, what the hell are you talkin' bout?" I could hear Big Jim from across the room. "I sold the boat last summer. What - have - you - and - Matt - done?" He asked broken and slowly.

"Uhh … nothin' Dad, I just didn't know you'd sold the boat."

My eyes were firmly fixed on Blake. I mouthed "What the heck?"

Blake covered the phone, "Dad sold the boat. We gotta move it back before Mr. Mötley Crüe down there sees it's gone."

Big Jim and Blake finished up on the phone, but even as good as Blake was at hiding details, Big Jim knew something was up. Blake and I devised a plan, I'd drive the old boat down to the neighbor's dock while Blake distracted him at the front door. It seemed solid, I mean as solid as it could be with Blake.

"I'm off. Give me a few minutes to get it started. Then when I hear you guys talkin', I'll start down to the dock." Blake nodded, and out the door I went.

What I couldn't see was Blake knocking on the big dude's door, but I heard enough. Mötley Crüe was thankfully a loud guy. He turned the radio down,

"Hey man, what's up?"

"I'm Blake. We have the cabin next door. That's a bitchin' Vette!"

"Yeah, it's all original. You a Corvette guy?"

"Well, I'd like to be someday. Right now, I just love to look at them."

"Right on. It's a great car. Alright, nice to meet you." The conversation paused, but Blake needed to keep it moving 'cause I was just now motoring down to the dock.

"Dude, you hear a boat?"

"Oh yeah, all the time around here. There're guys up and down this stretch of the river day and night."

"Well, that sounds like our old boat. What the heck?!?" Mötley Crüe took off running towards the back of the cabin. As soon as he cleared the back corner, his eyes locked onto me. The only thing that saved me from certain death was Blake and few well planted shrubs. Mötley Crüe tore around the side of his cabin and got hung up in some low growing holy shrubs.

"Son of bitch! What the heck are you doing! That's my boat!" Mötley Crüe hollered at me.

"Hey, I know, I'm just bringing it back!" That was the best I could come up with. Blake turned the corner expecting me to be a new dock piling, and thankfully kept quiet.

"Hey Blake, haven't seen you in a while. Your old boat was floatin' down the river, so I hopped on, and thought I'd bring it back. I found it down stream about a half mile. Can you give me a lift back?"

"Hey, Matt, sure thing. By the way this is my neighbor ... Sorry, don't think yall've met."

Mötley Crüe was a little slow to pick up on the cue. "Oh ... me ...yeah man Doug Jenkins. My friends just call me Doug."

"Nice. Well, I'm Blake. Matt's cabin is on down the river. I'll help him tie the old thing off. It used to break free from our dock all the time. You gotta watch that front cleat."

"Yeah ... okay. It's never done this with us. Somebody musta been messin' with it. I'll go check the camera tapes. We put them in after that break-in last fall."

Blake shot me a look of panic. "Ah ... I'm sure it just broke loose from a boat wake. Even though it's a narrow spot in the river, guys drive pretty fast through here."

"Yeah ... well ... Dad and me don't trust anyone up here. No offense ... but these jerks around here would just as soon steal from you than ask to borrow anything. We live in Texas but Jersey is still in our blood ... and we don't trust nobody in Jersey."

We didn't hang around for a thank you. In fact, Blake didn't get the food out of the fridge. We ran back inside, grabbed our bags and locked the cabin. Just as we were coming out of the front door, so was Mötley Crüe.

"You rotten jerks! I knew ya'll weren't nothin' but a bunch of thieves!"

Blake hollered at me "Time to go." Thank God his old truck started, and just as we were tearing out of the dirt drive, Blake yelled out "WE ARE JUST A BUNCH OF THIEVES. TELL WHO EVER LIVES HERE - WE ENJOYED OUR STAY!"

Mötley Crüe ran behind us a bit but couldn't keep up for long. "YOU BASTARDS! I'LL GET YOU!!!"

Blake looked back just as Mötley Crüe stopped running, out of breath and ideas. Then he spun around and started running back towards his Vette. "I'M COMING. YOU LITTLE BASTARDS!!" was all we could hear over the sound of Blake's old truck.

The roads around these parts aren't straight and long, there's lots of switchbacks and tight turns, as the original developer thought it would be packed with river houses, but the old scrubby brush country just wasn't that appealing to cabin dwellers, so thankfully for us, Mötley Crüe would have to know the area pretty well to catch us.

Blake tore across an open pasture gate and saved five minutes or so. Bouncing across the old pasture was hard on the stomach but great for putting some space between us. When we popped out the other side, we hit the highway and headed back towards town. We opted to push the tank of gas and take the back roads just after the first exit because even if Mötley Crüe wasn't that smart, his Vette was fast, way faster than the old truck.

Before long, Blake and I were well out of reach of heavy metal and his blue Vette, but if the old guy across the street spilled the beans, the jig would be up. As we drove home, I couldn't help thinking of all the ways this could go sideways. With Blake Ellis, you just never knew how the wheels could and would come off. When we hit the edge of town, the population sign for High Bluff greeted us, along with the reality we might be wanted criminals.

Big Jim was in the drive way when we pulled up, and said Old Man Walters had called him a few minutes ago. Old man Walters? I had no idea who that was, but Blake did.

"Oh yeah, we saw him this morning. Did he tell you?"

Big Jim just looked at Blake. "He did." Still nothing, just a blank stare.

"Yeah, it was great seeing him."

Big Jim, never letting on to anything else, just walked away. Before he opened the screen, he mumbled just above a whisper "He also said he took care of everything. Said, Jenkins has no clue who ya'll are. But *I* do."

Blake grinned and looked me. "I knew I liked that old guy."

Big Jim never spoke of that day again, but several months down the road, the Jenkins cabin was sold to some folks from San Antonio, and they had a brand-new river barge. When Blake learned the news, he just smiled and said, "Sound's like next spring's river trip might be *even* better."

CHAPTER 6

JUNE

THE FLIGHT OF THE WAMPUM

Camping in June is rather awful, especially in South Texas. Humidity, bugs, and heat are just a few of the unpleasantries one must deal with on a summer camping trip, but these are staples in the life of a Wampum Scout. The dreadful heat drapes over your body like a warm, wet blanket. Around High Bluff, the air is so laden with moisture you can almost drink it. At night, while trying to sleep, you feel sticky and just down right yuck. If you weren't already homesick, the uncomfortableness of the whole darn experience is enough to drive a boy mad.

Long about day three though, the elements don't soften but your psyche does. You grow used to the endless sweating, mosquito bites and nagging things crawling around on you, and after a few long days, you just settle in to enjoying the company. But camping trips this long only happen at the extended-stay two-week summer camp, so ninety percent of a Wampum Scout's camping trips are just pure, unadulterated misery, and this particular event was one.

Mr. Woolbuddy released the parking brake at precisely 4:30 pm on the first Friday in June, and we set off for Choke Canyon for our two night "pre-summer camp shakedown" stay. Choke Canyon was completed in 1982, so for us Wampum Scouts, it still had that fresh "new lake" smell.

The town of Calliham, Texas was now five feet under water and much of the outskirts were the state park where we'd be bedding down. We rolled in just about 6 pm and, before the sun went down, camp was set, and all of us were busy cooking our hobo dinners—beef and vegetables wrapped up tight in tin foil, tossed on top of hot campfire coals. This was the life of a Wampum Scout, free from home, cooking out under the open sky.

All of this worked like a NASA mission thanks to Mr. Woolbuddy. He was Jesus Maldonado's Scout Master when he went through the program, and that was about 1967. Jesus went through the Wampum Scouts with Mr. Woolbuddy, and now he was out there with us. He could cook anything, and I mean anything. When he was in Vietnam, he cooked all kinds of things from the jungle for the men out there with him. His claim to fame, though, was armadillo. Though it wasn't my favorite, most of the guys loved it. I swallowed one of those little armadillo whiskers when I first tried it and started gagging as I pulled it back up from my throat. I've never cared for it since.

That night, those who wanted it, dined on the finest hobo suppers and Mr.

Maldonado's armadillo on the half shell before falling asleep under the South Texas sky.

The following morning, Mr. Woolbuddy's bugle broke the calm and quiet. His own rendition of "Reveille" sounded the wakeup followed by his larger-than-life Texas drawl shouting, "RISE AND SHINE, BOYS!"

And that's how our first day on the lake began. A full day of canoeing, fishing and hiking lay before us, and by noon, we were all flat tuckered out. Mr. Woolbuddy and Jesus could see it in our eyes, so they agreed while the summer thunderstorms were whipping' up, we could all rest and eat. Perfect plan! The sandwiches, baked beans and chips went down quickly, and most of us headed to our tents before the rain started.

Plopped down along the banks of Choke Canyon, our tents were in the open 'cause down here the tallest trees are maybe twenty feet tall. This is brush country. Save for a few big old live oaks, most trees around here are mesquite, and mesquite trees provide more sap than shade.

Out in the open it was, and the first big boomer showed up fast. Before long, the rain was coming down in buckets. These fast-moving summer storms kick up after lunch, then, as fast they show up, they're gone. After about an hour, the storms had cleared and we all crawled out of our tents.

The steam after a summer rain can only be quenched by air conditioning or swimming in a lake, and seeing as how we were camping, the lake it was. We started gathering our things and then Garrick looked up behind us. "Hey … what the heck is that?"

"Oh, man … I've never seen anything like it before." Eugene said. Eugene and I had camped together for years and neither of us had ever seen a storm cloud that wide.

"It's like it's rolling, not floating like most of them," Eugene said.

Garrick chimed in, "I agree, look at that thing. It *is* rolling! We better batten down and hold on. Or maybe even go to the bus?"

"We're not going to the bus. It's too high. Besides, we got all those tire tubes up top and they'll just catch more wind. Listen up, boys, that cloud's rolling here quick and prolly has some wind with it. We're too far from the campground shelters so we're just gonna have to ride it out here. I don't want to be driving in the bus either, 'cause we just don't have any time," Mr. Woolbuddy said.

Just then the wind started whipping' up strong.

Mr. Woolbuddy gave the order. "TO YOUR TENTS! Put your sleeping bags on top of your body, and put your bags behind your head like a helmet! Do your best and don't die, 'cause I don't need that today. Okay? Well ... go on now and batten down!"

With that, Eugene and I tightened the tent's straps and hunkered down. The wind really started blowing, probably over 50 miles per hour in the gusts. Just as I tossed the sleeping bag over my head, a big gust hit and squashed our dome tent roof down to just about six inches above my head.

WHAP, WHAP, WHAP. The tent shook, a fierce wind ruffling up the side bottoms. Eugene and I did our best to spread out inside to keep the air from lifting the whole tent. The wind grew even worse, and, over the next few minutes, I wasn't sure how we stayed on the ground. Outside, it sounded awful, but all we could do was hang on to our bags and keep stretched out, 'cause if not, we'd be airborne.

It seemed like the storm lasted a long time, but it was only a few minutes. As the wind slacked off, we scurried out of the tent and, to our surprise, the bus roof was wiped clean of the tire tubes we'd planned on using that afternoon to float on. Tents and boy's clothing were scattered all over the lake shore. Marty and Nathan had blown all the way to the lake's edge but stopped short when Marty stood up inside and used his body weight to lean into the tumbling tent.

"BOYS! WE NEED A HEAD COUNT," Mr. Woolbuddy shouted then counted one, two, three, four … all the way to sixteen, but no seventeen! "Somebody's missin', who's missin'. DAMNIT, we don't need this today. *Who's missin'?*" Mr. Woolbuddy barked.

Our eyes scrambled around trying to figure it out. Eugene piped up "IT'S GARRICK, *GARRICK'S* NOT HERE, neither is his tent."

"DAG NABIT! He was in that tent by himself, wasn't he! Well … alright, let's start lookin' for him."

We all spread out in a long line and walked towards the shore, 'cause that's the way the wind was blowin'.

Before long, we all were standing at the water's edge. No Garrick. The storm was still rollin' across the lake and you could see it carrying the water straight up off the lake and tossing it over like a giant rolling pin. As we stood there, the magnitude of the situation hit Mr. Woolbuddy.

"Well boys, I ain't never seen anything like this. Let's all say a prayer for Garrick." We all bowed our heads, and the moment started to sink in. For a few moments, nobody spoke.

"Lord, please help Garrick. Keep him safe. Amen." It was a quick prayer, but we all knew it was from the heart. Mr. Woolbuddy was a Deacon at the First Baptist Church of High Bluff, and we were all sure Jesus heard his words, and not just Mr. Maldonado, but big Jesus.

We spread out along the lake shore and walked towards the road that went around the edge of the lake. It was several miles long and curved to the next cove where the state park headquarters were located. As Eugene and I walked, we could hear a truck coming but couldn't see it yet. Soon though, a Park Ranger's truck came slowly around the bend. Its flashers were on, and there in the back was Garrick's tent!

"What the heck? Is that Garrick up front?" Eugene asked then darted back down the road to tell the others.

"GARRICK'S COMING BACK WITH THE PARK RANGER. HE'S IN A TRUCK WITH HIM. HERE THEY COME!" By the time we all gathered round the truck, Mr. Woolbuddy and Jesus had sincere looks of relief on their faces.

"Boys, our prayers have been answered. Thank you, Jesus."

Mr. Maldonado smiled and said "You're welcome."

We all had a good laugh.

Garrick told us that when the storm was at its peak, his tent lifted off the ground breaking free from the stakes anchoring it down and tumbled across the lake. It rolled up against an outcropping of brush on the other shore. He got out and found the Park Ranger's office. We figured his tent skipped across the top of the water, gaining just enough altitude as to not drag down in the water. Inside, Garrick had the wherewithal to standup like a gymnast doing cartwheels and just kept going with it. He said, after a few spins, he got in a rhythm and just tried to keep it up.

"I figured I'd stop eventually but didn't want it to stop over the lake. I don't like to swim that much." Garrick said with a smile.

"Glad you made it boy, *awfully glad you made it*." Mr. Woolbuddy said giving him a bear hug. Even Jesus joined in the hug. Before long, we all joined in.

That night, Mr. Woolbuddy and the rest of us loaded up in the old scout bus and headed off for ice cream. Ice cream only happened on special occasions, usually when certain death was overcome. It was a grand evening, and certainly a spectacular day — the day a Wampum Scout flew, a day most worthy of ice cream.

CHAPTER 7

JULY

DICK PETERSON AND THE BOLL WEEVILS

It was a particularly hot summer, and a bumper crop of boll weevils was in full bloom across the south Texas cotton.

Dick Peterson was a respected Canadian talk radio host turned television journalist who had a weakness for enchiladas and south of the border fun. So, in an effort to accomplish yet another border town boondoggle, he envisioned a story for his television station, about the boll weevil infestation in High Bluff.

It's likely that as many Canadians knew of High Bluff as High Bluffians knew of Dick's beloved home in Toronto. In the early 1970's while on a Baptist Mission trip, Coach Wayne Small actually met Dick Peterson in Windsor, Ontario. Coach Wayne was fresh back from Vietnam and going through a religious phase. He was actually considering becoming a Baptist minister. The elders asked him to attend a mission trip in Detroit and see how he liked it. He'd be serving in a soup kitchen and visiting with the shut-ins. Noble work for a rising minister.

So, one night, while down at the soup kitchen, he met up with some homeless Vietnam vets who were hanging out at the shelter.

A few hours later, and well into some Pabst Blue Ribbon, Coach Small found himself kidnapped at a KISS concert in downtown Detroit. A few hours later, he was asleep on Dick Peterson's couch at a radio station across the Canadian border in Windsor. Rattled and clueless about the past few hours, he sobered up with Dick as his late-night radio show rambled on. Seems the vets thought it would be funny to load Coach Wayne up on beer and some other stuff he wasn't aware of, and then stuff him into Peterson's radio van while Dick was introducing KISS onstage. They just never imagined he'd wake up in Canada.

Turned out the two men became fast friends and stayed in touch over the years. When Coach Wayne took the coaching job in High Bluff, Peterson came to visit and fell in love with Tex-Mex food and a blonde-haired waitress named Marguerite.

Marguerite was a Canadian herself who moved to old Mexico to help save the Texas River Cooter turtle that she accidentally fell in love with during while getting her biology degree from the University of Texas. Along the way, she also fell in love with the food south of the border while doing her research project on the turtles near Matamoros. Somewhere between her 20's and 60's she forgot her way back home to the Great White North.

Marguerite made her home just across the border in Matamoros, and when she wasn't saving turtles, she worked part time at a cantina that claims to have the world's best enchiladas.

Years later, Coach Wayne was still teaching at High Bluff High School, but Peterson had moved on from radio to television. He hadn't made a "Texas Trip" in some time, but he and Marguerite talked regularly by phone and Dick was a generous donor to the Texas River Cooter Turtle Rescue, which was shortened to "Turk-Tur" around the Rio Grande.

The two men started plotting Dick's next visit, and as the summer boiled on, so did Peterson's appetite for enchiladas and a new visit to Marguerite. So, he worked up this big news story about the boll weevils to make it all possible.

The funny part was Dick Peterson had no clue what a boll weevil was—much less what it looked like.

His flight landed in Houston at 4 o'clock and a few hours later, he'd made it down to High Bluff in Coach Wayne's pickup truck. They had dinner on the road and tucked in early so they could do the news story in the morning to maximize their time in Mexico.

The sun came up quickly, and Coach Wayne helped Dick Peterson load all the camera equipment into the back of his truck. Off they went in search of some man-eating Boll Weevils.

Just past 6 am, they pulled in line at the Taqueria Guadalajara for some taquitos and coffee. Caffeined up, they pressed on towards Dale Johnson's monster cotton field just outside of town. As the sun crested the horizon above Nueces Bay, there was a smiling Dick Peterson in front of the camera.

"Behold, the bounty of cotton. But somewhere in this field lies a tiny, destructive killer."

Coach Wayne, standing just off the side of the camera, smiled and shook his head. "What … did I get something wrong?"

"Weeelllll ... noooo, not exactly, it's just that these boll weevils aren't all that small."

Coach Wayne wasn't lying. This particular summer hatched some of the largest boll weevils in Texas history.

"Oh, I see, so these are big boll weevils. Ha! Texas sized."

"That's right, little buddy ... they're big uns'."

Dick Peterson smiled again and confidently said "Take two."

"Behold, the bounty of cotton. But somewhere in this field lies a Texas-sized, destructive killer." As Dick started walking again, he paused deep in thought. "So, Wayne, just how big are these boll weevils?"

"Oh ... they're big. Biggest I've ever seen. Mean little suckers. You keep stompin' around out there and you'll find out. Them suckers will tear ... you ... up."

"Really? You messing' with me, Small?"

"No! I'm serious, these suckers are downright mean and ornery."

Peterson walked back to his starting position. In a slightly quieter voice, he said "Take three."

"Behold, the bounty of cotton. But somewhere in this field lies a Texas-sized, destructive killer." Peterson then picked up his foot and pointed down as he tippy toed a step and quietly started talking again. "I'm doing my best not to wake up the fierce predator, but somewhere in this field, they lie in wait … waiting and eating the cotton… and with it, the hopes of this Texas farmer."

Dick Peterson, now completely serious, stood up and, on his tippy toes, stepped back towards Coach Small. "How was that?"

"Oh … sounded good." Coach said.

"So what time is Johnson showing up for his interview?"

Coach Small checked his watch. "Should be anytime now."

"Great, I don't want to give them a lot of time to find us." Peterson said, checking over his shoulder for any angry boll weevils.

Coach Wayne, enjoying Dick Peterson's growing concern over the boll weevils, pressed on with his duties of assistant producer. "Can I help you move the camera, Dick?"

"Great idea, let's set it up behind your truck. Johnson and I can do the interview on your tailgate, like real Texans. It'll look perfect!"

"Oh … good idea." Coach Wayne lifted the camera and tripod and had it set up just as Mr. Johnson's truck appeared in a cloud of caliche dust from the west.

"Hey, here comes Johnson. Let's get ready," Dick Peterson said, more nervous now than usual.

After getting Mr. Johnson positioned on the tailgate, Dick Peterson walked back over and sat down. Neither man was small, so as Dick took his seat and the truck's shocks settled a bit, Coach Wayne instinctively lowered the camera, keeping the men in frame.

"I'm here now with Dale Johnson, the owner of this cotton farm. Dale, tell me, are you afraid the boll weevils?"

"Well … I am. They'll eat up everything we have here if something ain't done about 'em."

Peterson pressed on. "What scares you the most about them. Is it their size? Their teeth?"

"Teeth?" Johnson asked. "Well … I guess it's their size, and just how many of them there are. I swear at night and about mid-morning, it sounds like a sawmill runnin' around here. Them little suckers just tear through a field."

Dick Peterson shook Dale Johnson's hand and stood up. He walked right over to the camera, and said to the invisible audience inside its lens, "Come with me."

Coach Wayne, with a slightly surprised look on his face, moved the camera back to the edge of the field and when Dick Peterson yelled "Action," he started filming.

"Here I am now back in the field … a field filled with terror, where an angry pestilence, fueled by the devil himself is running out of control. I, Dick Peterson, will now attempt to catch one."

Coach Wayne looked up from the camera's view finder and threw a confused glanced back at Dale Johnson. The two men smiled a bit and tilted their heads in the way a cowboy watches a city fellow mount up on a horse. Dick Peterson, in all his glory, loudly stomped his feet and flapped his arms up and down.

Much like the winged Albatross walks, Dick Peterson traipsed about Dale Johnson's cotton field in search of the man-eating boll weevil he'd dreamt up. Coach Wayne and Mr. Johnson were fighting back laughter but did their best to keep quiet, all the while darting glances in disbelief back and forth to each other.

Finally, Coach Small hollers out, "Here comes one, Dick! Just behind you."

Dick Peterson swung around to confront his certain death, and in the process tripped on a cotton root and fell flat on his back. "YAAAAAAAHHHHH! It's got me. IT'S GOT ME, I'M CERTAIN!!!!"

Coach Small and Dale Johnson shot laughs out like a shotgun blast as they ran over to help Dick Peterson.

Peterson's arms and hands were batting off what they thought were imaginary boll weevils, but, to their surprise, Peterson was actually covered in boll weevils laying there in the cotton.

Now, boll weevils can't bite a human, but, sure enough, he was covered in weevils. When he'd fallen, they must have gotten stirred up, and to Peterson's amazement, he was surviving the attack.

"Lookee here, Dick. They are—*no kidding*—all over you."

"Yup, never seen so many on one man." Dale Johnson plucked them off his own pants as he ran one back over to

Dick's camera and explained. "This right here is the largest one I've ever seen!"

Peterson, never one to waste a good moment, rose in a cloud of dust from the Earth like Lazarus and slow walked towards the camera, plastering his weevil-infested face in front of the lens. He gripped Dale Johnson's hand. "That's right, folks, the largest one he's ever seen. Dick Peterson, reporting from Dale Johnson's farm on the Boll Weevil crisis in Texas. Cut!"

And with the story now in the can, Dick Peterson immediately wiped away the weevils and exclaimed "Who's ready for enchiladas?"

Coach Wayne and Mr. Johnson, still laughing about Dick Peterson's fall in the field, couldn't resist, so Coach Small says. "You sure you don't want to walk back out there and dig up a few more man-eatin' boll weevils?"

"No more than you'd like a Pabst Blue Ribbon," Dick Peterson fired back with a sharp grin.

The enchiladas that night were some of the best they'd ever eaten together, and Dick Peterson's story about the boll weevil crisis in Texas went on to win a national news award in Canada. The award came with a cash prize and matching grant to the charity of Dick's choosing. Cheers to good friends, great enchiladas, and a very happy Marguerite and a few lucky Texas River Cooter Turtles thriving in the new Dick Peterson Wing of the Turk-Tur Rescue Center.

CHAPTER 8

AUGUST

DANCING, DUNKIN' & LAKE LIFE

The summer before my senior year, Dad said me and my buddy Eugene could use the boat to ride over to the big Saturday night dance at Fiesta Marina. Showing up to a summer dance at Fiesta Marina was a rite of passage, and arriving by boat was a brave decision on my dad's part. I mean seriously, what sane adult thinks it's okay to let two 17-year-old boys take a new boat to a dance … on a lake … with actual water in it … and come back home at night … in a boat … on a lake?

I'd grown up on the water, and my father trusted me implicitly with the boat. But when you factor in the stupid things boys do when hormones get involved, this was the equivalent of running with some of those freshly sharpened Ginsu knives you see on late night TV.

Me and Eugene shoved off from the dock at 8 pm sharp so as to be fashionably late and arrive at 8:30 pm when the band got started. Chrysanthemum Dunlop and Marie Olivier, sophomores from nearby Orange Grove, were meeting us there. It was going to be a fun night of dancing and root beers, but the fancy kind in brown bottles.

"Lake sure is smooth tonight," I said to Eugene as we left the cove by my grandparents' house.

"Sure is ... smooth like my boots."

"Are you boots smooth?"

"Sure are. I've got smoooooth boots and smoooooooth moves," Eugene said before he started laughing. The thing I love about Eugene is his laugh. He's like a wind-up toy, just turn the key a few rounds then get ready for an ear-to-ear grin followed by laughing that would make a hyena blush. Seriously, I've never heard anyone laugh like Eugene. When he gets going, he goes all the way. Completely unafraid of how he looks or who hears, he just belts out a belly laugh and before long it spreads around the room and nobody but Eugene knows what started it.

When we were about four years old at our Junior Wampum Scouts meeting, he thought he heard his cat fart, and laughed so hard about it, Brooks Davidson had to go change his pants. When they finally got Eugene calmed down enough to talk again, they asked him why he was laughing so hard. When Eugene blurted out "'Cause I thought I heard my cat fart," the whole darn room, including Eugene, busted out with snorts again. Poor little Brooks just turned around towards the front door and went home, 'cause his mom didn't have any more pants in her bag.

Like then, Eugene was giggle-ready tonight, and we'd just barely left the dock.

The whole way, he kept slidin' his smooth boots to the imaginary songs playing in his head.

"I'm gonna be movin' like this ... then I'm gonna spin Marie around, and maybe dip her right under the mirror ball, if it's on. She's a GOOD dancer, so I'm gonna get to really have some fun out there. What about you? You ready?"

All of a sudden, I could feel him staring me down. Everybody in High Bluff knows that if I'm dancin', there's somebody holdin' a gun to my head, or the punch has been spiked. When God was handing out talent, he gave me absolutely zero dancing ability. I mean none, not one iota. If I start, people ask me to stop. It's that bad. Eugene knew this better than anyone. Countless hours, he'd try to help, and countless hours, he'd just start laughing again.

"Sure ... I'm gonna try. But you know me and dancing," I said.

"I do ... maybe you ought to just stick to the slow stuff."

"Perfect … thanks Eugene. I'll just sway — I'm good at swaying."

On the horizon, rising between the waves, a neon beacon shone bright, a lighthouse built from Lone Star and Shiner beer signs. Seeing this meant the safe harbor of Fiesta Marina was just around the bend, and waiting beside the dock, would be Chrysanthemum and Marie.

I'd already planned our approach, because the last thing any kid who's grown up along the water wants to do is bungle up the arrival. One bad move and I'd be bouncing off every boat in the marina.

We were not "lake boat people." We were Laguna Madre boat people, and our boats were built for fishing the flats, so they didn't have keels or v-bottoms. They're flat as an iron skillet. With any amount of wind, our boat won't hold course at slow speeds, it just blows with the wind. If you jam it in reverse, she'd slide to the left uncontrollably from the propeller torque. It's tough but doable with lots of practice and I'd had lots of both with Dad watching over my shoulder, but I still didn't want to screw it up.

Everything was looking good. I had a light wind off my starboard side, and it was just enough to help hold me to the downwind dock. Perfect, I thought as we turned into to marina's canal.

"Hey ... Matt ... are you watching this?"

"No, what?"

"Dude, this big cigarette boat on the right! Jerk's nosing in and is going to cut us off."

Eugene was right. Some drunk guys with a boat load of drunk women were plowing their way into the canal from the opposite direction. They weren't paying any mind to me, much less the line of pontoon and bass boats coming in behind us. One old man in the pontoon boat in front of us started hollering. Lots of fingers were raised, and several kids learned some new words, but the jerk just kept on coming.

He slid right into the dock we were cued for, and rammed it so hard, he had to pull back in. Now the whole canal was rocking with the waves from his wake. Eugene knew it wasn't going to be easy when his smooth boots started sliding around the deck. He fought hard for some traction and to grab hold of a line tied to the front cleat.

"Boy ... some jerk huh?!?"

"I can barely stand up," Eugene hollered back.

I was focused now on watching the fallout from everyone else. The pontoon boats faired pretty well because they were dug into the water. The bass boats had deep v-hulls, but our 22-foot flat-bottom was like a bar of soap on wet ice. I was doing my best to hold it steady, but because of the waves, the only place left to dock was about the middle of main pier. It was really tight and everything was now stacked against me. The girls spotted us because of the commotion and waved, walking towards the upcoming disaster.

"Hold on to that the line, Eugene, and get ready to push us off these other boats."

Eugene just shook his head. "Don't worry, I'll crawl around if I have to, 'cause these boots won't let me run."

We were both too focused to laugh, but miraculously, when I made the turn, our skiff just glided right into position. Beaming, Eugene stepped off and tied us up to the dock! We made it like pros.

As we walked away, I asked Eugene if he'd double checked the knot. He nodded and said "Ay-ay Captain." Eugene has a way of completely living in the moment. He can be in a great party or with a dentist drilling into his tooth without any Novocain. He doesn't discriminate. He's always present … he's all in with the good and the bad. I've always admired his ability to be completely in. Tonight was no different.

Chrysanthemum and Marie giggled as Eugene grabbed both their hands, sporting his Alfred E. Newman grin and laughing about something only known to him. He kicked the swinging doors with his boot and we were in.

Through the wooden floor, you could feel the beat of the band, and the shuffle of the dancers' boots sliding across the fresh cornmeal and baby powder sprinkled on the hardwood floor. The silhouettes of cowboys nursing beers and lies were backlit by the neon signs. Christmas lights crisscrossed the whole ceiling, and a spinning mirror ball in the center of the room set the pace for the slow dances.

Humans have gone to great lengths to protect rare birds and sea creatures with nesting grounds and heavily guarded estuaries, but places like Fiesta Marina are equally as important for the survival of Texan culture. A hallowed, native redneck breeding ground, Fiesta Marina was responsible for untold generations of pickup truck buyers and heaps of cheap beer sales.

As the beat drove on, Chrysanthemum and Marie had us on the dance floor, spinning and two-stepping the night into our memories. At the end of the evening, we bellied up to the bar for a cold root beer float, then Eugene and me had to ready our exit.

We walked Chrysanthemum and Marie out to their truck then turned back for the boat dock.

"Man, what a night! WHOOO, what fun!" Eugene hollered with a smile.

As we passed by the back porch of Fiesta Marina, two college girls shouted down to Eugene "HEY...Why ya'll leaving so early?"

His eyes nearly burst when one of the girls blew him a kiss. "We saw you dancin' in there. Come spin us round one time before ya' go."

Eugene didn't even ask. He hopped the porch rail and hooked their arms and was gone! I made my way back inside to watch just as the band kicked off a cover of Travis Tritt's "T-R-O-U-B-L-E."

Eugene kept both those girls spinning like two plates whirling on top of sticks. He'd toss one around while the other one orbited just outside his reach. Good Lord, he could dance. In and out, back and forth, he really showed those college girls how to spin across the floor. When the song ended, he gave them both a dip, and they came up and kissed his cheeks.

I knew then, he was going to explode, and so did he. He tipped his hat and as quickly as he hopped the dance floor rail, he was back outside making his way to the boat.

The girls started hollering again "HEY... don't run off. Let's keep on goin'."

Eugene shot them his grin again and we kept moving towards the boat. To our dismay, those college girls followed.

"This isn't in the plan. Dude, we just need to get to the boat," Eugene said with a glow in his eyes and step so quick I could hardly keep up.

Darting down the dock, I scanned the darkness for our boat, but it wasn't there.

"Dude ... what the hell?"

"I know it was right there!"

"You saw me tie it up. Jeez!"

Just outside the veil of yellow bug lights on the dock, bobbed our boat, all by its lonesome. The knot Eugene had tied in his haste must have slipped, and now, set a drift into the darkness, was our ride home.

The college girls hollered down towards the dock. "Well, now ya'll got a problem. Come on back in and dance. There're more kisses, too."

Eugene was perplexed, and I knew the only way to get this solved was going to involve someone getting wet.

"Well … shoot." Eugene said under his breath, then glowing through the darkness came his grin. In one fluid motion, he stepped out of his boots, and beamed back towards the college girls, "Ain't gonna be no dancin' til after a little swimmin'." Eugene kicked off his pants and shirt then bent over to lay down his hat, and started laughing. He dropped his skivvies and flipped off the dock into the dark water.

When someone drops all their clothes and jumps into water around a party, it has the same effect as a yawn. Everyone seems to do it. Those college girls started shouting, and like a dam busting open, a solid stream of screaming cowgirls poured out of the swingin' doors and straight down the dock, and into the lake.

In about fifteen seconds, Eugene was floating buck naked in a sea of college coeds and a few old hippies. Before long, the confused cowboys and gawkers showed up to watch the spectacle of youthful exuberance. Eugene eventually grabbed the bow line, and swam our skiff over to the end of the dock.

Looking up and grinning from the water's edge, Eugene handed me the line. "Well ... I don't think anybody noticed my knot came undone. Mind grabbin' my clothes?"

We both had a little laugh as I tied the line up around the cleat and went back for Eugene's pile of laundry and hat. Eugene slid bare-bottomed into the back of the boat, and with a gentle nudge off the dock, we drifted in silence towards the darkness of the night, watching the whole drunken, naked flotilla of college girls and a few hippies devolve. Mother Nature and cheap beer no doubt turned Eugene's good-natured dip into a few more pickup truck buyers.

As we slowly motored away from Fiesta Marina, we both laughed just like that time in Junior Wampum Scouts.

"My goodness, THAT was a night!" Eugene said, as I cleared the no wake buoy, poured on the throttle and set course for my grandparents' lake house.

We didn't say much on the way back, but we sure did laugh as Eugene's grin lit the way home.

CHAPTER 9

SEPTEMBER

HOUDINI THE COW

The Baptist Men's Group often takes part in charitable causes, and nothing could be more charitable in High Bluff than the annual High Bluff High School's Heifer Club end-of-year sale. The students work all summer long raising their project animals. Then, in the fall, they auction them off to the highest bidder.

Some use the money to help launch their lives, but most use it for beer money during their first run at community college. Either way, all the money goes to the kids and, in the South, that's a big thing. This year, the Baptist Men's Group had their mind made up on purchasing little Carmen Sanderson's bull, Kaw-Lija.

Named for the famous wooden Indian in Hank William's song, Kaw-Lija the bull was an impressive animal but still considered a sport model by Texan standards. Kaw-Lija was a soft bull, a gentle animal raised on a bottle and often walked about town on a hot pink lead with fake diamond studs lining the handle and halter. Kaw-Lija did have a Native American-looking neckerchief that was always around his neck. The reds, oranges, blacks and blues of its geometric designs stood out against his dark black hide.

Carmen named him Kaw-Lija because when he was just a tiny tot, he'd sit down on his rear end and rock back against a wall. There he'd sit, like a dog begging for a treat with his front two legs up in the air. When he first did it, she thought the little bull looked like the wooden Indian in Mr. Presley's barber shop.

Running home and telling her father the story about her young bull sitting on his rump, Mr. Sanderson, said "Sounds like little Kaw-Lija is quite the bull." The name stuck.

It might have been officially fall, but, that afternoon, the south Texas sky was beaming down, and the metal roof of the sale barn was so hot it would fry a fly if one was brave enough to land on it. Inside, there must have been two hundred folks gathered to watch the lunchtime auction. Ladies were fanning themselves with the event program, hoping the spray in their high hairdos wouldn't melt or nab a passing mosquito, and all the while the men were sweatin' through their starched white wrangler shirts.

The natural smells of a hot sale barn mixed in the air with the aromas of snuff, dime store Stetson cologne, and the occasional hint of Chanel Number 5. When Bull Harlan pulled up with Reverend Arbuckle, they circled up around the back of the barn where all the trucks with trailers parked. Attached to Bull's old Ford was a small red-painted, metal two-horse trailer. Emblazoned on the side of the trailer in white paint with gold and black accents was the word "Rocket." Rocket was Bull's old ropin' horse who'd passed away several years back. but, in the years to come, many of the Baptists Men's groups outings, where a trailer was needed, were covered by Rocket's old ride.

The front of the old trailer had a small window where Rocket used to poke out his head and get some fresh air when he and Bull were parked.

"It's gonna make for a comfortable ride for Kaw-Lija's last trip," Reverend Arbuckle said getting out of the old Ford.

Carl Jacobs walked in with purpose, and his checkbook, making sure he beat Arbuckle and Bull inside. He took his bidding flag and grabbed a seat about halfway up, so the auctioneer could see him. The first cow out was a fluffy all-black Angus. She was just the right size. However, the Baptists Men's Group was set on Kaw-Lija. But if they were outbid, the question remained, should they have a spare? This one was just right.

Carl spun around in his seat and motioned to Bull and Reverend Arkbuckle who were still coming around the corner to take their seats. When Carl poked out his hand, the auctioneer called him out "Carl!? You biddin' on this animal?"

"Oh no, your honor. I'm just tryin' to get Bull's attention."

The crowd started laughing.

"Carl, I ain't no *judge*, I'm an auctioneer! Keep yuh' hand down till ya' want to spend money."

"Yes, your honor." Carl followed.

It was a lively auction, and the animals were going for big money. One big ol' bull named Titus brought nearly eight thousand dollars, and, with that kind of bidding, the Baptists Men's Group would be out of luck. When little Kaw-Lija poked his head out of the chute, Carl Jacobs stood up and held up his bidding flag. He was a small bull, and certainly not the most desirable, but he was perfect for their upcoming benefit bar-b-cue. The auctioneer started the bids at five hundred dollars, and Carl just kept his hand up. Some old rancher sitting across the aisle was also bidding til he saw Carl standing up.

The old fella nodded and put his hand down. Carl turned and grinned at Bull and mouthed "We got him!"

Sure enough, the auction ended at twenty-five hundred dollars! A handsome price for a small bull. That money would cover Carmen's first year at the community college and fill the bellies of lots of folks buying bar-b-cue plates in a few weeks. At the end of the auction, Carmen walked Kaw-Lija out to the trailer and tearfully said her good byes. When she took off little Kaw-Lija's lead, he nuzzled her head, and when she sniffed a tear back, he let out a little moan.

Carmen walked out of the trailer and helped Bull Harlan close the rear the door. In silence, Reverend Arkbuckle handed Carmen the money. His lips were pursed and a tear ran down his cheek too. They hugged, and with a stiff upper lip, Carmen walked back towards the barn.

"Well ... we got him!" Carl Jacobs said, reaching out his hand to shake Bull's. "It was pretty touch and go there for a minute, Bull, but we got him. Yall have a safe trip back." As Carl turned around towards his car, a loud kick came from inside the little red trailer.

Bull's brow shrunk, and his lips tightened. Another kick, this time harder against the door, then the sound of metal swinging could be heard above all the ruckus. Bull walked around back to see what was going on, and out popped Kaw-Lija. He'd jumped over the back gate 'cause Bull had left the split top down for air flow seeing it was so hot.

Carl Jacob's eyes grew to the size of coffee cups even though he was safely in his car. He rolled down the window on his Buick, and shouted "Bull's got loose! The Bull's got loose!"

"Damnit, Carl, we know. Get out here and help!" Bull Harlan fired back. Carl grinned then sheepishly waved, easing away with his window up. Bull grabbed a rope from behind his seat, and swung it over his head. With every orbit, the lasso got larger.

With a gentle toss, Bull Harlan laid the rope right over Kaw-Lija's head and everyone in the parking lot applauded. Old Bull pulled Kaw-Lija back towards the trailer, but this time, he wasn't planning on going back in so easily. He started chuffin' and snortin' the closer he got.

Bull hollered over to Reverend Arbuckle. "You're gonna have to help me, Reverend. I know you love those rodeo clowns, so here's your shot. When he gets in, we're gonna slam the whole ramp shut, top and all, and you're gonna have to help me hold it closed till I throw the latch."

"Okie-dokie, Bull, I'm ready. I'm cowboyin' up," Arbuckle said with a grin.

Bull approached with a calmness that came from somewhere deep inside. He steadily led Kaw-Lija up the ramp and, in a flash, jumped back as Reverend Arkbuckle threw the door. Kaw-Lija kicked the door so hard, his hoof prints poked through metal.

Arbuckle screamed. "HE'S GONNA KICK THROUGH! Come on and get that latch!"

"Hold it closed. It's comin' down another inch, and I can't get it," Bull shouted back.

"We need more men!" Arbuckle fired in return. Both men's shoulders were getting pounded by the increasing swifter kicks from Kaw-Lija who was now madder than a cornered rattlesnake.

One final kick and both Arbuckle and Harlan were knocked to the ground. As the gate crested the top and fell towards them, the men rolled to safety narrowly missing the whack of the steel. Inside the little red trailer was a snortin' slobbering' pissed off bull nobody had seen before. His eyes glinted red as he scratched his hoof against the trailer floor and darted his head side to side, throwin' spit while sizing up the souls he was about to take.

"Damnit, Arkbuckle, we gotta get that ramp closed!"

The two men found their bravery and raced back towards the ramp in a last-ditch effort to close it. Kaw-Lija lunged and raced from the back of the little red trailer and right up the ramp. Like a scene from a children's book, Kaw-Lija jumped over the edge of the ramp, with feet tucked back, just like the cow leaping over the moon. He hollered in mid-air, and a clump of white slobbery goo fell from the sides of his nose and lips.

When Kaw-Lija's hooves struck the dirt, he started buckin' and chasing any person not already running towards safety. By now, the crowd of cowboys were scattered, and Bull and Reverend Arkbuckle were hiding behind the barn door.

Bull waited for Kaw-Lija to turn his head towards the trailer, and then he ran out into the parking lot and grabbed his rope. Reverend Arbuckle remained frozen behind the gate, not entirely from fear of the loose bull, but knowing this was a job for someone with experience.

He could lather up a sermon, but he couldn't lasso a lathered-up bull.

Tuck Jamison, a cowboy from the Kingsland Ranch, jumped down from the railing around the sale barn and hollered at Kaw-Lija. Tuck raised his hands and made all kinds of noise to distract him and draw him over his way.

Meanwhile, Bull Harlan opened up a pen just inside the barn and held his rope at the ready should he need it. When Tuck took off towards the pen, ol' Kaw-Lija followed him right on inside. They slammed the gate and let him cool off while they all had lunch.

After the cornbread, ham, and beans settled, Bull backed up the trailer to the pen and the other cowboys built a makeshift shoot to funnel Kaw-Lija into the trailer. It worked great, but as Bull and Reverend Arkbuckle pulled away from the barn, Kaw-Lija started lunging again inside the trailer.

This time, Bull watched in his rearview mirror as Kaw-Lija, now spittin' mad, tossed his front legs and head through the tiny window in the front of the trailer! Now in a full up sweat, Kaw-Lija wiggled and moaned his way to freedom. When Bull slammed on the brakes, it gave Kaw-Lija the extra momentum he needed, and just like a fresh newborn baby, he popped right through window and into the bed of Bull Harlan's old Ford!

"Dag-nabit, he's LOOSE *AGAIN* Arbuckle! He's a regular Houdini, this cow! Never seen anything like it!"

Kaw-Lija was trying to stand up but couldn't get any traction on the slippery metal truck bed. He just laid there in a fit of rage, chuffin', snortin' and kicking so loud you could hear the metal of the tailgate buckle and bend.

At this point, Carmen Sanderson herself had driven back to the sale barn to help. "Kaw-Lija ... I'm here!" she shouted as soon as she and her dad stopped the truck. She ran from across the parking lot just as Reverend Arbuckle cleared the passenger side door.

Kaw-Lija, now on hoof, turned sharply, and his eyes, clouded by adrenaline, tried to lunge for Arbuckle, but again his hooves failed him on the truck bed. He slipped but noticed the sliding rear window open to the cab. Kaw-Lija tucked his head inside and started pushing his way toward the interior of the truck.

It was at this point, Bull Harlan had enough. "What the *hell* does this damn bull think he's doin'!" Bull Harlan reached inside and grabbed Kaw-Lija by his horns and with one final pull, he drug the raging animal out the door, and shot him with his pistol.

The whole parking lot gasped. As the gun shot echoed, but the screams of Carmen Sanderson were louder. She ran around the other side of the truck where her eyes met Bull Harlan's.

"*You... YOU* shot him? He was *just* trying to get inside with you, cause that's where he was *used* to ridin'! You're all just a bunch of maniacs!" Carmen was furious, but in the end, everyone else knew Bull didn't have a choice. Reverend Arbuckle pried himself out from behind the railing where he'd been crouched and walked over to Bull.

"Poor little Carmen's really upset ... but I suspect she'll get over it. I just can't believe the damn thing fit through that window. I thought he was gonna kill me where I sat."

Bull didn't even look up. He motioned for Arbuckle and Tuck to help him drag Kaw-Lija back into the trailer, so they could get him over to Nardela's Butcher Shop before closing and the heat got to him.

The crowd just stood and watched. Bull unwrapped Kaw-Lija's neckerchief and walked it over to Carmen's truck where she was crying on her dad's shoulder. He held it up, then laid it on the hood. As Bull walked away, her dad nodded and mouthed *thank you*.

"Come on, Arbuckle, let's get Houdini to the butcher." Bull said as they loaded up, and pulled away.

This year at the Baptist Men's Group's annual charity bar-b-cue, nobody mentioned Kaw-Lija. Hank William's and Charlie Pride's versions of the famous song were both played as an unspoken tribute in his honor, but among the Baptists Men's Group, it was unanimous — they all thought Houdini was a much better name.

CHAPTER 10

OCTOBER

THE DINOSAUR CHICKEN

It was a crisp fall Saturday morning when the phone on our living room wall rang.

"Hello?" Dad said, motioning me to turn down the TV. I could hardly make anything out across the room, from the muffled and tinny sounds of the telephone receiver.

"Jim, this is cousin Garth from out in Arkansas. How you?"

"Did you say Garth?"

"Yes, sir, we met long time back in Sherman, when Paw and me drove down."

"Oh, yes, I remember. How are ya', Cousin Garth?"

From what I could gather, Dad's cousin, Garth, along with another cousin, were driving down from Arkansas to deliver an old car they'd sold to a collector in the Rio Grande Valley. The car was a 1935 Packard Super 8 that had been stuck in a barn since the land owner disappeared sometime in the 1960's. Dad's cousin bought the barn, and then sold the car off. It was apparently worth a considerable price to this fella down south of us, and now they were arranging a bit of a family reunion along the way.

Cousin Garth and a second cousin, twice removed, Thomas Jefferson Burleson or "Jethro" for short, were leaving out Monday morning and arriving at some point several days later. They were planning to stay down at the High Bluff Motor Lodge and make use of the midnight special on their lighted fishing pier.

The day Garth and Jethro arrived, we could hear them coming quite some time before they turned the corner. The muffler on their old truck must have fallen off around Bug Tussle 'cause it sounded louder than a top fuel dragster. The old '73 Dodge Ram looked like it had been beaten with a baseball bat and maybe rolled down a hill at some point —possibly in reverse. The two men were both grinnin' as they pulled up in front of our house.

Just under his breath I could I hear my dad say "Good Lord."

"Cousin … Jim?" Garth asked as he crawled out from the driver's side door that had been tied closed with an old rope. Garth and Jethro were both wearing new gas station sunglasses that still had the price tags dangling down.

"How ya doin' there, Jim? Good to see you," Garth said, as he patted my dad's back. He took off his white sunglasses with fake diamond accents, and looked at the price tag, "I bet you're wonderin' why I left this tag on? Well … I want Kristie Jean to know I paid good for em' when I give em' to her back home." With a wink towards my mom, he said "Carole Sue …

goodness it's nice to see you, too." He picked Mom up and spun her around.

"Why ... Garth, I think this might be the first time we've met, but it's mighty nice to see you, too," Mom replied as he sat her back on her feet.

We all walked inside but cousin Jethro didn't say anything. He sat down on the couch and smiled. Every once in a while, he'd nod politely but never a word spoken.

"Sure is a nice place you have here, Jimmy. Kristie Jean and me's planning on puttin' in an indoor laundry later this month with some of this here car money. That ol' washin' kettle and wringer get pretty cold in the winter months." He paused then laughed. "Nah! I'm just kiddin', not about the indoor laundry, just the wringer. We're not uppity. Kristie Jean still likes the kettle, but she's also been a dryin' line kinda gal since we got hitched. Says the fresh air makes em' feel cleaner, and a dryin' line won't pinch yer fingers. I don't mind it, but, Lordy, it's hard to put on frozen step-ins."

The three of us, didn't really know how to respond. Jethro didn't either. He just kept grinning every once in a while and lookin' around.

Mom served up some coffee and we sat around a bit, while Dad and Garth got reacquainted. That evening, the plan was to meet up for supper at the Country Kitchen for a store-bought meal. Garth and Jethro were headed back for a long nap, so they could fish out on the motel pier after we ate.

When we rolled up to the Country Kitchen, Garth and Jethro were parked out front in the old Dodge. The doors creaked and moaned like a heifer calling a calf. "Evening, Carole Sue. Howdy-do, cousin Jimmy." Garth said as he walked up.

"Garth, Jethro, ya'll come on in here. Gonna need a good meal in ya' to fight all those fish tonight." Dad held the door and in we went.

San Patricio is a dry county, so the only place you can buy a drink is the country club, and the Cotton Blossom, which is just over the county line. But the

Country Kitchen would let you bring in your own beer or wine if you wanted something to sip with your meal. Dad brought in some Coors Light and offered one to Jethro and Garth who both gladly accepted. With the "schh" of the pop top, Jethro's eyes looked at ease.

Ben Anderson, who owned the Country Kitchen, walked over. He's a tall man with dark brown hair and a full face, supported by cheeks that said he'd have a beer, or six if offered. Mr. Anderson who heard the "schh" sound of the Coors can opening, slapped Dad's back with his bear paw of a hand. "Jimbo, good to see ya'. Who's visiting … and don't mind if I do." he said, grabbing a beer.

Just then the front door swung open and the bells above it jingled as Bull Harlan, Coach Wayne Small, and Reverend Arbuckle walked in. "My goodness, they'll let anyone here," Reverend Arbuckle announced.

Before long, our table grew from five to eight, so Dad ducked out to the Maverick Market for a few more beers.

With every "schh" sound, I noticed Garth and Jethro seemed more at ease, and long about the time Garth's number six opened, that's when it happened.

"Ya know, Jimmy, this sure has been fun seeing ya'll and meeting' yer friends here. This car money's really gonna help us out 'cause it's been a pretty lean year for Jethro and me. Them emus didn't work out like Jethro and me had hoped."

"*Dii-noo-sarr Chickens*, them things is di-no-sar chickens," Jethro explained with his arm bent like a snake standing straight up. When he said *di-no-sar*, he moved his hand back and forth like the head of the giant bird or Steve Martin walkin' like an Egyptian.

When someone speaks, who's not said a word in your presence, and suddenly blurts out *di-no-sar chicken*, they have the floor. That night, Jethro did.

From the end of the table, Coach Small was the first to pipe up. "What *exactly* is a dinosaur chicken, Jethro?"

"Oh … you joke, but when you stare into the eyes of one them thar cold-hearted-killin' birds of thunder, with talons ready to rip yer' heart out … that smile wouldn't be on yer' face, Mister. These 'birds' aren't birds at all. They're *dii-noo-sarr chickens*, di-rect descendants of the ty-ran-o-sawrus rex. As God as my witness, Mister, them things is the meanest creatures around."

"Well … there, little buddy, I didn't mean no offense, I just never heard the term," Coach Small said as he cracked open another beer. He passed that can to Jethro, and just like that, Jethro kept talking.

It seems that on a hot day this past August, right at sunset, Jethro and Garth were driving past a farm near the eastern border of Missouri when they saw a sign that read "FREE EMUS — BRING TRAILER". Well, they had the same trailer they had with them on this trip, and it was empty, too. So, they swung back around and headed towards the farm.

Jethro had read an article one morning in the Ozark Trader, while having breakfast down at the Biscuit Wheel, about how emu farming was a real money maker. The article touted how profitable emus could be and how little work they required—two things Jethro liked.

The only problem was, Jethro didn't know anything about raising emus or even what they like to eat. He and Garth pulled up to the farm house where they'd seen the sign, and a small man in overalls with a planter's style straw hat raced out the front door. The little man's beard tips blew up in the wind as he ran alongside their truck motioning them to follow him.

"C'mon … c'mon up this way!" The little man shouted. He kept pushing his finger-smudged glasses back up his nose running farther and farther back until finally he came upon a giant cage.

"Don't look like nothing's in there, Jethro, maybe we come too late," Garth said.

"Ya'll swing round, and back yer' trailer on up to this gate. Let yer' trailer door on down, and then I'll run em' on in. Then ya'll get the hell outa here — I don't ever wanna see these birds again ya' hear!"

"Yes, sir." Jethro said as he hopped out to help Garth back up the trailer.

Garth leaned out the window and whispered, "You sure bout' this, Jethro?"

"Sure 'bout it? No … but how hard can a buncha birds be to raise and kill? Come on back now. I'll guide ya' in."

The truck sputtered as Jethro walked back alongside the red glow of the taillights towards the emu gate. The little man had disappeared into the darkness, but once in place, Jethro eased down the trailer door, then hollered out, "Send em'!"

Seconds turned to minutes, nothing moved, no sign of the little peculiar man. No sounds at all except the idling engine of their old Dodge truck. Jethro went over and sat down on the wheel well of the trailer, and started whittling on a stick. Garth anxiously looked around but didn't speak. The two men just waited.

Then, somewhere in the darkness, they heard the man start screaming. "HEY ... get ready!! They comin', they *comin' mad'n* FAST!"

Jethro jumped up and ran around to the back of the truck. He motioned to Garth to get ready to back up once the little man cleared the gate. Jethro left just enough room for the tiny man to jump clear. Then Garth would seal up the space between the fence and the trailer so the birds couldn't escape.

Like a rabbit over a fence, the little man came whizzing around a scrubby tree and spotted the gap Jethro had left. He shouted out "Much obliged" and cleared it in a flash. Garth spun the tires and backed up the whole rig, sealing the gap. When Jethro turned around, the little man had done run all the way back up to his house.

"Thank ya'll much, and good luck!" The little man shouted from the safety of his front porch, then he walked inside and slammed the door. He even turned off the porch light! It was back to silence.

Jethro shrugged and chuckled under his breath, "Okay" and gave a wave towards the now dark and empty porch.

Then like the sound of a thousand bait fish jumping for their lives in front of a shark, the noise of thundering feathers and giant bird feet filled the night sky. A piercing screech echoed, and an onslaught of dust, feathers, and the most terrible noises and smells you ever experienced came round the corner.

"It looked like a herd of stampeding, feathered buffalo!" Jethro didn't hold back while telling this part of the story. "Their wild eyes shown red in the taillights, eyes of killers, I tell ya'! They slammed into the trailer walls, screeching louder and louder, clawing and crazily bouncing around so much we couldn't figure out how to slam the door."

Garth shouted out above the noise, "GRAB THE *ROPE*".

Jethro, snapping out of the combat-like panic, yanked on a rope tied to the trailer door and slammed it shut. Garth eased the truck forward while Jethro brought down the locks. Above the screeches from inside, he hollered back to Garth, "All clear!"

Garth popped the clutch and pulled forward so Jethro could close up the fenced area's gate. When he hopped in the truck, he turned to Garth. "Well, that was interesting." The two men drove back in the moonlight with the windows down, and as soon as they hit the highway all the screeching stopped.

"How many them things you reckon are back there?" Garth asked.

"I have no idea, probably at least 20 or so."

"They was bigger than I thought they'd be — and meaner," Garth said with a reverent and serious tone.

"Bigger than *you* thought, hell them things is *dii-no-saurs*!" Jethro said with his eyes still wide open from the shock.

The next morning, Jethro patched up the fencing he had on an old axis deer pen he'd built a few summers back, and then ran out the pigs he'd been keeping inside it. This would become the emus' new home.

About eleven o'clock, they dropped down the gate to the trailer and the beasts were set free. There was no commotion or anything, they acted like they owned the place and just strutted down the ramp of the trailer.

Until the last one got up to leave. The stud of the pack was a rough one. He was a least a foot taller than the rest and had one eye that was blind and milky white. His beak was chipped, and, if he could've shot whiskey and smoked Marlboro Reds, he would've.

"We're gonna call this one Rex," Jethro announced.

In late October, Jethro and Rex came to an understanding. Every day, Rex patrolled the perimeter of the pen. The others stayed calm, as long as he was calm. The birds ate well and were putting on weight, so much so, it would soon be time to harvest a few for market.

Jethro had been reading up on the process and was handy with a blade. So, when the time came, he talked it over with Rex, walked in and picked out a nice bird to harvest. Quick as a fiddler, Jethro dispatched the bird and dragged it out through the gate under the watchful eye of Rex.

"That damn Rex just kept pacing back and forth by the pen's edge as I carved up his buddy," Jethro said, moving his hand back and forth like a snake head. "He's cold-blooded, I tell ya'! *Cold*-blooded."

That evening Jethro and his bride, Tammy, prepared some of the bird, and the rest they tossed in the fridge to sell down at the farmers market the next morning.

"Now the meat is really lean, damn near no fat at-tall. But Tammy did a fine job of fryin' it up. In fact, we had so much, and she'd cooked it up so good, I got over served that evening." Much to everyone's discomfort, Jethro then went on to explain how the extra lean meat even had some undesirable effects on his body. Something about breaking out the cheap whiskey the next night to "get everything moving again."

"So, let me get this straight, Jethro…" Coach Small interjected, "You just walked in and *KILLED* one of them dinosaur chickens in front of that crazy one, and then drug out the carcass and slaughtered the damn thing right in front of him? *Jeebuz!*"

"Well, I wanted him to know I was the boss," Jethro said with a chuckle. "And ya know Coach, the whole time … here he was … back and forth … back and forth." Jethro made his arm move back and forth like the head of a cobra snake. "Just the weirdest damn things you ever seen. But you know, after I hauled out what was left of the bird I'd harvested, things changed." Jethro said.

"The birds apparently talked that evenin', and decided if they didn't make a move, they were all going to wind up like their friend…"

As Jethro spun his yarn, Coach Small, Bull Harlan and even Reverend Arbuckle were drawn further and further in. I couldn't help but be drawn in, too.

"Well, the next morning me and Tammy woke up and could tell something was different. Them birds looked a parading army of North Ko-ree-an soldiers."

They were all marching the perimeter of the pen, two or three at a time, in line-abreast formation. The crazy one, big Rex, stood dead center staring right at Jethro and Tammy. His big white milky eye, and his one good one, were laser locked onto Tammy and Jethro. As Jethro moved closer to feed them, they all, on Rex's cue, screeched so loud Jethro said the neighbors telephoned up the hill to check on them.

"For days, if we walked out to the car, they'd screech. They'd screech when I took out the trash. They'd start jumping' round like fighting cocks, spurs flying, them big ol' nasty talons digging into the dirt, kicking' up dust. Whoooo, I tell you, they were figuring on killing Tammy and me.

"That night, while watching the Halloween special of Hee Haw, just as ole' Buck Owens started singing a spooky version of Streets of Bakersfield, I looked out the winder behind my chair 'cause I heard something scratching on the house. I didn't see nothing, so I grabbed my rifle and pressed my face and hands up against the winder as to see out into the night. Still nothing, and the scratching had stopped. I said, 'Tammy, *Tammy* ... be real quiet like, and come over here. See if you can see anything.'"

"What we lookin' fer?" she said.

"Well ... I don't reckon I know, probably an old coon or something," I replied.

Jethro's voice got low and slow. "There we was, both looking out when WHAM—right there on the glass! Ole' REX's big white witches eye pressed up against the winder! He screeched so loud I *pissed my britches*, and I ain't too proud to admit it. Tammy done fell back and grabbed my old 30-30, and shot that damn bird straight through the glass winder!"

"It's time fer *KILLIN'!*" Tammy shouted in a cold-blooded voice, "*TIME—FER—KILLIN'!*"

"Jeebuz … I guess so!" Coach Small blurted out. Now by this point, the whole Country Kitchen had gathered round the table for the rest of the story. Jethro got real quiet and lowered his head a bit, and spread his hands out over the whole table.

"We knew they'd breached the pen, so as Tammy went out with my 30-30, I grabbed the scatter gun. She was already towards the pen when she hollered back, 'On yer left!'

I fired into the night, and dropped one of the big ole sows. She fell down and started floppin' and hollerin' and that's when Ole' Rex poked his head around the corner of the cabin."

"Damnit, Tammy, it's REX! He's still alive!"

Jethro said Rex was like a ninja. He tiptoed around the back of the house and then jumped on top of Tammy's Mercury Sable. He started clawin' at the roof paint and screeching as she fired away on his pack. Tammy was so pissed she knew he was trying to draw her out, so she just kept killin' his kin.

It must have looked like a cartel shootout. Feathers, blood and dust were flying everywhere. Emu guts splattered Tammy's face and her favorite house coat was now stained with the blood of the fallen. But, undeterred, they both killed all but six of the evil dinosaur chickens that night.

"I raced over to help Tammy. The motion sensor kicked on the porch light and lit up Rex on top the Sable. He was screechin' and carrying on like one of them vo-loss-a-raptors from the movies. I pointed my 12-bore at him, and he dropped his head down so he could see me with his good eye.

That's when he started making this clicking noise and turned his head around to see Tammy who was walkin' over. Still clicking inside 'is throat, but not screeching, he started making this low-down thumping sound in his chest. The other five dii-no-saur chickens swung round behind him, but they was all silent. He let out one last screech then jumped up about 10 feet in the air and ran off up the hill into the night with all the rest of them!"

"What the hell? You didn't blast his butt into next month?" Coach Small fired.

"Naw ... truth be told Tammy and me was out of shells, and I think he knew it. He could uh killed us at any moment, and we knew that, too." In almost a reverent tone, Jethro continued. "He let us live that night ... scariest Halloween I'd ever have."

"Ho-Lee-She-Taky-Mushrooms!" Reverend Arkbuckle shouted. "I mean, seriously Ho-Lee-She-Taky Mushrooms!"

"Okay now, calm down there, Arkbuckle, there's kids around," Bull said.

"Oh, for Heaven's sake Bull ... the man just stared down the face of a satanic dinosaur chicken, and his wife... Ol' Scarface herself ... slaughtered most the herd bare handed in a house coat ... that is

MOST worthy of a HO-LEE-SHE-TAKY MUSHROOMS!"

That night not only did I learn a few new words, I also learned I never wanted anything to do with emus.

As the night wrapped up, and Coach Small lit up a cigar and sipped a scotch, that appeared out of nowhere. Coach leaned forward with a smirk and asked "Ever see any of em' again there, Jethro?"

"Well … every now and again, about this time of year, when the harvest moon comes out. I'll see a shadowy figure way up yonder on the hill—just silently moving along—slowly. I know it's him … and he *wants me* to know it's *him*." Jethro moved his arm slowly back and forth, "The dii-no-saur chicken."

I'm not sure if they fished that night or not, but the next morning, they pulled by the house. They didn't get out, on a count they already had the doors tied shut, so Mom just handed over some coffee and taquitos for their drive. We said our goodbyes and as they pulled away, just before they turned the corner, Cousin

Garth blew the horn and the old trailer squeaked right on cue. And the last thing I saw as it rounded the bend was ol' Jethro movin' his arm back and forth out in the wind.

Mom mouthed "The dii-no-saur chicken."

CHAPTER 11

NOVEMBER

THE DEER HUNT

Jude rolled in from work and hollered as he came through the door, "Stormy, if we're going, we gotta go right now."

Her bedroom door immediately flung open, "Dad? You're not changed? I'll meet you in the truck. Make it quick."

"Okay, I see how this is gonna be."

For years, Jude had taken Stormy fishing and dove hunting, but deer season was all about Jude and his dad. Last year, when Stormy turned ten, she cornered him while he was skinnin' his first buck of the season. If he didn't take her on the next hunt, she'd never forgive him.

"Dad, if you don't teach me to hunt, who's gonna do it?"

"Well, baby girl, we'll go next opening day, but you're gonna need to be a little bigger to handle your own rifle, and you're gonna need to be good enough to hit a deer at 200 yards. That's gonna take some time and work…"

"Well, when I am ready, I wanna *BE* ready, and if you don't start takin' me, I ain't gonna be ready."

That summer, Jude came home with a nice Browning .22 for Stormy to use for target practice. It even had a scope. It was a much nicer gun than Jude's trusty iron sight Winchester, but only the best for Stormy. For her birthday, instead of something froufrou, Jude bought her some camo pants with a matching jacket and new boots. Stormy looked like a model from the Bass Pro catalogue. She was ready to go hunt with Jude. Every weekend, she and Jude fired 25 rounds through her gun. She practiced from a sitting position, from a tree stand, and laying down in the weeds in the prone position.

"Baby girl, if you was just a little bit bigger, you'd be able to handle this rifle, but ya' can't hunt with that .22 -- but, boy, you're gonna be ready when you get bigger."

Jude did his best to prepare her for every situation, and by the time November rolled in, she couldn't wait to see everything happening for real, but most of all, see her hero daddy Jude in action.

November 5th was opening day, a Friday. Jude left early from work so they'd have enough time to walk in to the stand and get setup before the golden hour. With Stormy already in the truck, Jude practically jumped into his pants and camo top. He grabbed his trusty Winchester, along with his grandad's Buck Knife, and ran out the front door.

"Come on, Dad, drive!" Stormy was ready and couldn't wait to finally get into the woods with her dad. When they pulled up, they sprayed themselves down with scent block, then walked in towards the stand. From here on, Jude and Stormy would communicate only with the hand signals they'd been practicing.

Two fingers up meant to hush up, full hand meant something's moving, and if they started pointing, it probably meant a Game Warden or a deer. As they settled into the wooden shooting house, Jude couldn't help thinking about how great this was.

"Stormy, I can't believe we're finally huntin' together. Baby girl, I'm one happy papa," Jude said as he settled into the shootin' chair, and cracked open a fresh pack of cookies. "We're gonna need to wait till just before sunset for the big-uns so just ease back and get comfortable. Thin Mint?" Jude asked holding up his favorite lucky deer hunting cookie. "You know I only hunt with Thin Mints, them Girly Scouts seem to cook deer bait into every Thin Mint. Don't know what it is, but I swear they help call in the big-uns."

Soon the afternoon turned to early evening. A cool and crisp fall breeze was blowing up the gentle hill the shooting house set on top of, and just as the sun was starting to get low in the mesquites that lined the food plot, Jude popped in his twelfth Thin Mint.

Jude raised up his hand. Stormy squinted. Was it a squirrel or the rustling sound of a deer about to emerge from the tree line? The sound of scrub brush rustling and small sticks crackling seemed amplified in the stillness of the evening. Soon, a baby deer hopped out of the scrubby brush between the trees. It looked around and lowered its head and plucked up the green winter rye grass that painted the open space of the food plot. It was probably six months old or so, a happy-go-lucky little sucker. With every nibble of the grass, its signature white tail shook with delight, oblivious to Jude and Stormy a hundred and fifty yards away.

A few minutes later, the momma cautiously poked her head out into the clearing. She carefully made her way out, checking behind herself the whole time. The does know the bucks are crazy this time of year. Actually, they're just outright insane.

"Baby girl, she knows bucks are like a bunch of teenage boys at the prom. For every pint of blood, they have two more pints of stupid juice pumping in their veins," Jude explained with less than a whisper.

"Hormones make bucks and boys do stupid things, and this is the season for both. Grown men playing Rambo, and dumb bucks behaving like boys. A man's world is often a dumb world, and does and women know it," Jude added with a wink.

The doe kept looking over her back. With every chew, the doe's head would pop up to search the sage brush for the crazed buck. Mother and child stood together eating the fresh sprigs of green, but momma deer was wound tighter than a cheap watch in a bucket of magnets.

With every rustling leaf or crackling stick from a squirrel bouncing around, the mother would stop and look. Just over the hill, a murder of crows called, and Momma kept looking back to their direction because she knew that could mean a buck. With every nibble, Jude would look down at his Thin Mints. He really wanted another one, but knew he couldn't make any sudden moments.

If the deer moved slightly, Stormy took note, never missing a breath or tail twitch. She was completely consumed by the moment. "Papa, if we're gonna kill a deer, your tummy's gotta settle down. I can feel you *wantin'* Thin Mints from here. Stop," Stormy whispered.

With a grin from Jude, there was a rustling sound from behind them, and the blind blocked the vision of whatever it was. "It's probably just a squirrel. Hear how it's jumpin' around? Deer don't jump. So, hand me a Thin Mint."

Stormy's lips flattened and with a sour look on her face, she grabbed Jude a cookie.

The minutes crept forward like trucks in a traffic jam. With every breath came the renewed promise of a big one. Tension like this is why folks hunt. As evening draws its shades of darkness, the big ones loom near. They are the creatures of the margins. Everything they do seems to exist in the margins of Mother Nature's world. They live in the edges of daylight and darkness, showing themselves only where the shadows play. Momma deer's head spun hard left and didn't lower. She focused only on the woods. As a male dancer takes the stage in a high brow ballet, the Muy Grande entered the arena, his head high as he took steps filled with purpose announcing his arrival. You could hear him saying, "I am here. I have arrived—gaze upon me!" If deer could be arrogant, this guy fit the bill.

Jude grinned as he lowered his right eye towards the iron sights. His right hand slipped down near the trigger, and in one motion, slid the safety into the fire position. Focused and ready for the Muy Grande to turn broadside, Jude steadied the bead and slowed his breathing. As the Muy Grande continued to prance, Jude's right hand retreated from the trigger and his eyes darted away from the sights, and took their attention to his leg, then back to the buck. Stormy took a quick glimpse and spotted the problem. *Ants!*

Jude's beloved Thin Mints were covered in Texas Reds. The big nasty man-eating fire ants had found his Thins and were eating them. But that didn't stop Jude. He doubled down on the deer and again slowed his breathing as the ants marched on. Jude muttered under a whisper, "Don't pay no mind to them, Stormy, focus … focus … he's settling down now." Jude set his chin on the stock of the rifle. "Focus …."

Just then the Muy Grande stopped and posed for the perfect kill shot. He turned broadside and raised his head, with one eye turned straight towards Jude. "Well … look at that, it's like he sees me. look, baby girl … it's like he's begging me to take a shot!" Jude's right hand slowly pulled the trigger, and just as the gun fired, Jude hollered out "YOW!!! JEEEEEEZ. YOW, YOW! *Kill em'!*"

Stormy jumped up from her seat and looked around at Jude, thinking something had misfired on the gun. "WHAT IS IT,

DADDY?" she said with panic in her voice.

Jude's left hand was swinging faster than a bull's tail on flies, and his feet were stamping around. "It's these damn fire ants! They're *KILLING ME* ... one just bit me right down there!" Jude pointed towards his unmentionables, "OHHHH ... it hurts ... ohhh, ohhh, OHHHHHHHH."

Stormy couldn't hold back the laughs. "Daddy, it's those damn Thin Mints. They ain't so lucky now! You just missed that buck 'cause of a cookie! *Daaaannnng!*" She giggled.

The Muy Grande stood just off to the side, in a fog of disbelief. It seemed to enjoy the folly of Jude's discomfort and Stormy's laughing. The shot had completely missed him.

"Well, Daddy, we ain't takin' Thin Mints next year. Nope," Stormy explained as her laughter turned into outright hysterics.

"Baby girl, don't you laugh. We need to be quiet so we don't scare the deer. Look … he's still here."

"Oh sure, Daddy. 'Cause you hollering YOW, YOW, YOW clearly didn't scare him! Come on, let's get you outta here."

Stormy gathered up their stuff, and helped Jude limp back to the truck, laughing the whole way. "Ole' Thin Mint Jude … the finest hunter in Texas!" Stormy said laughing with her head on his shoulder. "I love you, Thin Mint, but next year, we're takin' something else, something fire ants hate."

CHAPTER 12

DECEMBER

THE LIVE NATIVITY

It was to be the most spectacular live nativity the Baptist Men's Group had ever hosted. Even better than the 1974 production when a young college girl named Shelby Goldstein played the Virgin Mary. The Baptist Men's Group hired Shelby along with her two brothers to play Joseph and the shepherd boy the very day their family moved to town from New Jersey. The thought of having an authentic Jewish girl playing the Virgin Mary—in South Texas—was just too good to pass up. When Deacon James Herbrich heard the news, he ran out and rented the string of billboards between High Bluff and Corpus Christi. Normally they advertise for a biker bar where clothes are optional. The place, and its signs really gets the dander up on the good Christian folks in town, but Deacon James was able to replace just one word on the first billboard to get the point across.

Lit with giant the flood lights the words "LIVE JEWS" shown bright on the side of the highway. The next billboard down the road read "AUTHENTIC LIVE ANIMALS" followed by "ONE NIGHT ONLY" and finally, "SEE IT ALL AT THE LIVE NATIVITY - FIRST BAPTIST HIGH BLUFF".

Deacon James' wife Miz Nancy nearly wrang his neck when the first sign came into view. "My Lord - JAMES!" Miz Nancy gasp nearly knockin' her perfectly vaulted hairdo off her head.

"It's real nice ain't it!"

"Nice? My Gawd James, you can't say "LIVE JEWS". I mean seriously! You CAN-NOT say THAT! Ya'll gotta take that down!" Miz Nancy was already gettin' out of the truck, ready to climb up and rip the sign down herself. "I mean seriously! It's insensitive—and *vulgar* 'cause we all know what it says underneath. Now, don't tell me you rented the other one up yonder," she said with one eye brow arched higher than a church steeple before she pressed him more. "You know, the one held up by that 22-foot-tall slutty woman with her leg hiked up?"

"Now, now, Nancy, I'm not sure I know what you're referrin' to, honey?" James sheepishly replied, tryin' to calm her down.

Nancy grabbed her bible out of the truck door pocket and whacked him upside the head. "The hell you don't! I know damn well you and every other Baptist Men's Group Member knows what the *hell* I'm talkin' about—and now you gotta get this sign down, James Herbrich!"

While it was impossible to pull down the sign, short of a dynamite blast by tomorrow, the billboard did catch a lot of attention, in fact, it even made the evening news. When the local Rabbi was called in to smooth things over, the sign became legend. The idea of having authentic Jewish actors, plus a live donkey and several sheep were what really put the whole event over the top that year.

This year, they were going all out again. After much discussion, and seeing how the FBI shut down the bar and dismantled the 22-foot-tall "slutty lady", there would be no billboards.

It would however be Shelby Goldstein's daughter Melody playing the Virgin Mary, and Marty Tibbets as Joseph, along with a world-class set built by a real Hollywood set designer. When the movie business moved to Austin, several Hollywood types bought beach houses and Duke Winslow was one of them. He'd designed sets for several big action movies but fell in love with the Coastal Bend when he worked on *The Legend of Billie Jean*. Duke was a big dude. He might have worked in Hollywood, but he was straight up Texas stock.

"We'll put the manger over here, I'll build the walls out of foam, but they'll look like stucco, and for the manger, we'll use some re-claimed olive wood. That stuff might even be from Jerusalem. Probably be able to sell it afterward for big money to some yuppies up in Austin," Duke offered to a few of the Baptists Men's Group volunteers standing around the vacant field beside the church.

"Well, Duke. Is this gonna be an okie dokie place for the production?" Reverend asked, walking over from his office.

"Yes sir, gonna be just fine, Reverend. We're gonna build the set facing this direction, so the setting sun will paint a dramatic backdrop each night, and over there, you'll have plenty of extra parkin'."

"Extra parking? *Wow*! It's really gonna be a big un," Arbuckle said with a giddy and slightly star struck grin.

Coach Small and Bull Harlan had met Duke one day down at the Dixie Cream Donut stand where they were having breakfast. The three of them struck up a conversation, but it was Coach Small who actually floated the idea of having Duke build the set.

"Ya' know Duke, you'd be perfect for helping us with our little Christmas pageant over at the church. We build this live nativity thing every year, but the buildings are usually just crappy old pallets from the port and a few burlap sacks tossed over em'. We could really use a true craftsman … a man of the trade like yourself. It'd be great to have your input."

Surprisingly, Duke said yes and got right to work on the most elaborate live nativity set High Bluff had ever seen. It had a fountain in the village center, buildings that looked straight from Bethlehem. Plus, it had room for all the live animals the Baptist Men's Group could wrangle up. Shelby's brother, Chris, had moved away, but since this was such a big deal for their family, he'd agreed to fly down from his home in Alaska and bring along his newborn son to play the baby Jesus.

The thought of having authentic Jewish actors again, plus live animals and a Hollywood quality set had the whole town at a bursting point. It was gonna be so big that the Methodists volunteered to move their annual Singing Christmas Tree right next to the set for an all-out High Bluff ecumenical Christmas spectacular.

"Holy smokes, I just can't believe it. It's really a Christmas miracle." Reverend Arbuckle crowed during his Sunday sermon. "Ya'll just have to be here next week. Just like Coach Small says … it's gonna be one big do-dah!"

On opening night, Melody and Marty looked just like Mary and Joseph, and LeRoy the donkey, the most well-mannered donkey in south Texas, played the part perfectly. The three entered from stage left just as the Methodists hummed an emotional rendition of *No Room at The Inn*.

Somber and reverent, the Holy family made their way to each door, only to be denied by the finest over-actors in High Bluff. In glorious fashion, Wanda LeFavor opened one of the doors to what was supposed to be a home, and pointed so ferociously towards the manger that Marty's younger brother cried out, "What a mean witch." It was just loud enough that his five-year-old voice could be heard, and misunderstood by the whole crowd.

His mother was embarrassed, and swore to those around her that he just has trouble pronouncing his double-u's, but it did get a laugh. Undistracted and still looking forlorn, Joseph and Mary, on the back of the donkey, turned toward the manger.

Back stage, completely unbeknownst to the entire town of High Bluff, a catastrophe was unfolding. The little Jewish baby flown in from Alaska had fallen ill on the flight, and his father, Chris, was distraught.

"As bad as we want him to play Jesus tonight, this cough is getting worse by the minute, and now he's running a fever." Chris exclaimed.

"Must have picked something up on the plane. Poor little fella," Eula Davis said with her hand over the microphone on her Stage Manager's headset. "We'll just have to figure something else out and fast." Eula added, looking off into the distance.

Just as Mary, Joseph, and ol' LeRoy the donkey knelt down by the crib, the Methodist slid into their next somber number, "Oh Cold, Oh Cold Bethlehem, How Cold" which they sang in tight four-part harmony.

A spotlight shone down on the Holy Family, and right on cue, LeRoy the donkey knelt down beside them. High Bluffians, none the wiser, sipped their hot chocolate and apple cider while marveling at how much Mary and Joseph resembled the characters on the color pages in the backs of their Bibles.

"It's just uncanny ... I mean, they look just like them," Maggie Scaborsik whispered to Gladys Olsen, her bible study classmate.

"She sure does. I'm just gobsmacked by it all. Gobsmacked, I tell ya," Gladys whispered back.

Meanwhile just behind the manger set, Brackston Hunter was helping wrangle the other barnyard animals and the three camels for the wise men to ride in on. Brackston loved animals and never went anywhere without his own pet monkey, Kevin. Eula Davis looked up and just beyond her, stroked with a yellow ray from the spotlight shining in between the cracks of the set walls, stood the perfect replacement for little baby Jesus—Kevin, Brackston's Capuchin monkey.

In slow motion, Eula raced between the goats, camels, and wise men adjusting their cloaks and gifts. She glided on her tip toes like a calorie-enhanced ballerina, almost floating towards Brackston in perfect time to Mrs. Biggles' high note. Surprised, Brackston looked at Eula now standing nose to nose.

"Give me Kevin. We need him," Eula commanded with no time to spare.

"Huh ...?" Brackston said confused.

"I need Kevin to play baby Jesus tonight. The kid's sick, so he's in. He's the only baby Jesus we got."

"Uhhhh ... okay."

Faster than a bass to a worm, Eula had little Kevin wrapped in the Jesus swaddles, and plopped into the hands of Agnes

Brown, who was reprising her role as the angel soon to appear at the manger.

One year, the Baptist Men's Group had written into the script a simulated live birth, but during rehearsals, it scared some of the children so badly, a few of the girls actually considered becoming nuns. So, ever since then, Agnes Brown has had the privilege of playing the angel who tastefully delivers the baby Jesus to the crib.

Marching in with all the reverence of a battlefield commander, Agnes Brown carried Kevin, the smiling capuchin monkey onto the stable set. Bathed in the same glowing yellow light that Eula first saw him in, Kevin beamed as he was carried to the manger. His little smile and glistening brown eyes shown brighter than any of the other actors, and, as the audience applauded, he grinned even wider. His little eyes batted at Mary and Joseph, and everyone cooed. Once he was laying in the manger, the Methodists launched into their birth of baby Jesus medley. "Oh, Holy Night" was the first up.

Mary gently stroked Kevin's head, and then picked him up to cuddle him closely. Kevin was perfect!

Even Gladys and Maggie smiled. "I think that's little Kevin, the monkey. Sumthin' must have happened to the Jewish baby," Maggie said quietly.

"Well, I think little Kevin is doing great," Gladys whispered back. "What a *little cutie*."

As "Oh, Holy Night" was wrapping up, Mary placed Kevin back into the crib just as the timpani drum began to roll. Bawng, bong, bawng, bong, bawwwnnng sounded the timpani, and the Methodist's Singing Christmas Tree burst into "Joy to The World". Randy Jensen, right on cue, lit Kevin up with the glowing white-hot spotlight. It was incredible … at least for all of the High Bluffians. Gasps and applause could be heard all the way to the Country Kitchen downtown.

But Kevin winced noticeably from the bright spotlight, and the thunderous applause was clearly making him distraught. I'm sure the slightly off-key singing didn't help the situation, but little Kevin pitched and rolled in the manger, and then he started shimming out of the swaddle. As soon as his little arms were free, he burst out like a fart in a whirlwind, screaming the whole way as he ran straight up the wooden column in front of the manger.

There was more gasping from the crowd, and in the back behind the set, Eula Davis muttered over her headset microphone to the tech team, "Sounds like we got ourselves a sit-e-atchun. Ya'll keep an eye out for little Kevin. He's on the run."

Little Kevin wasted no time getting out of the limelight and scampered onto the very top of the village set running along the ridge line of the fake buildings. He jumped from the stable to the little house where Wanda LeFavor had been so rude, and it was there that his tiny feet got tangled in a strand of wiring running along the top for the stage lights. Sparks flew up behind his feet, looking like pyrotechnics at a rock-n-roll show, but those sparks fell down and lit a nearby hay bale ablaze.

The flames made a whooshing sound as they leapt faster than Kevin from building to building. LeRoy the donkey had enough, and, when he bolted from the manger scene, full on pandemonium broke out.

"Come on, Bull. We gotta do somethin'," Coach Small hollered to Bull Harlan as they watched in disbelief.

"Damn right, Coach. We gotta stop Kevin before he burns the whole damn town down," Bull replied.

Kevin was now running down the risers on the Methodist's Singing Christmas tree, which was surprisingly still belting out "Joy to The World" as the flames now ravaged the Bethlehem village set mere feet away. Mrs. Biggles never missed a note of "repeat the sounding joy" and for that matter, neither did the rest of the choir.

As the camels, sheep and goats scattered across the rear parking lot, and

"Joy to The World" came to its closing verse, off in the distance you could hear the wailing sirens from the fire trucks of the High Bluff V-F-D. Everyone was aghast at the scene.

Just as Kevin bolted back towards the set, his foot wrapped around a cloak on one of the wise men running off to fetch his camel. It must have been ten feet long, and, as he zoomed back up the wall of the flaming set, the cloak caught fire, too.

Kevin looked back, and he was now completely surrounded by flames. His only option was to jump backwards and try to make the tippy top of the Methodist's Singing Christmas tree. It was the very spot where Mrs. Biggles, dressed in her shining star costume atop the tree, was belting out the final note.

Kevin spun around. All of High Bluff watched his tiny outstretched hands and the flaming cloak in trail, blazing like jet engine afterburner. In slow motion, his hands grappled the wind, and his face filled to the brim with hopes of a safe landing on Mrs. Biggles Christmas star styled hair.

But somewhere between his great leap of faith and the dreams of a safe landing, Coach Wayne Small drew his .45 caliber pistol and fired a shot right at Kevin's chest. The muzzle blast echoed over the choir, and little Kevin's eyes—oh his sweet little brown eyes—darted away from Mrs. Biggles, and locked onto the bullet. His tiny hands once grappling the wind flew straight up tossing his hopes to the heavens and setting his body into a downward slow-motion fall. He, along with the flaming cloak from the wiseman, fell into the blackness behind the now crumbling set still ablaze.

The crowd was silent, the song was over, the set was now completely engulfed, and the Live Nativity dreams of the Baptists Men's Group were in smoldering ruin.

"You did the only thing you could do, Coach." Bull Harlan said with his hand upon Coach's shoulder. "If he'd made that jump, half them singing Methodists would be on fire by now, too."

"I know, but I loved that little monkey," Coach Small replied with one tear plinking down his cheek. "I hadn't loved a little monkey like that since Vietnam. We had one as a pet in our hooch over there. Gosh darn it …." Coach Small was a whimpering wreck. Between the rampant fire, the gun blast, and of course … his having to shoot little Kevin, Coach Wayne's memories from 'Nam had overcome him. While Coach and Bull were hugging it out, a real High Bluff Christmas miracle was taking place.

Brackston was frantically looking for Kevin in the smoldering ruins of foam and wood that was once the Bethlehem village. Just there on the edge of the set, he found him, lifeless with his little hands pressed into the dirt like a murder victim ready for tracing on a New York sidewalk. Brackston knelt down, and, with tears in eyes, he gently picked little Kevin up and hugged him one last time, and that's when it happened.

Little Kevin opened his eyes, and hugged Brackston back. "Holy smokes, ya'll! He's ALIVE! He's ALIVE!" Brackston shouted. He ran forward into the crowd still in shock from what they'd witnessed. "KEVIN IS *ALIVE,* ya'll ... HE'S ALIVE!" Brackston explained holding a smiling Kevin up for all to see.

"He's alive ... the monkey's alive" was all you could hear rolling over the crowd in whispers. Folks were still in a reverent mood from all the shock, but just over those whispers, Mrs. Biggles still atop her post on the Christmas tree softly started into *Silent Night.* Before long, all of High Bluff was signing with her. It was our Christmas Miracle, the night Coach Small shot Kevin, our little Jesus monkey, and he too, seemingly rose from the dead.

It truly was a Christmas Miracle, and all in all, the most spectacular live nativity we'd ever seen.

www.ingramcontent.com/pod-product-compliance
Lightning Source LLC
Chambersburg PA
CBHW060524080526
44586CB00012B/601